RICHARD M. NIXON

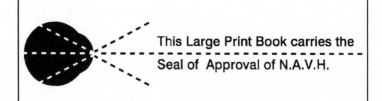

This Large Print Book carries the
Seal of Approval of N.A.V.H.

THE AMERICAN PRESIDENTS

RICHARD M. NIXON

ELIZABETH DREW

ARTHUR M. SCHLESINGER, JR., GENERAL EDITOR

THORNDIKE PRESS

An imprint of Thomson Gale, a part of The Thomson Corporation

THOMSON
GALE

Detroit • New York • San Francisco • New Haven, Conn. • Waterville, Maine • London

LIBRARY OF CONGRESS CATALOGING-IN-PUBLICATION DATA

Drew, Elizabeth.
    Richard M. Nixon / by Elizabeth Drew.
      p. cm. — (The American presidents)
    Includes bibliographical references and index.
    ISBN-13: 978-0-7862-9902-7 (lg. print : alk. paper)
    ISBN-10: 0-7862-9902-9 (lg. print : alk. paper)
    1. Nixon, Richard M. (Richard Milhous), 1913–1994. 2. Presidents —
United States — Biography. 3. United States — Politics and government —
1969–1974. 4. Large type books. I. Schlesinger, Arthur M. (Arthur Meier),
1917–2007 II. Title.
    E856.D74 2007b
    973.924092—dc22
    [B]   2007026672

Published in 2007 by arrangement with Henry Holt and Company LLC.

Printed in the United States of America on permanent paper
10 9 8 7 6 5 4 3 2 1

For Arthur Schlesinger

CONTENTS

EDITOR'S NOTE

THE AMERICAN PRESIDENCY

The president is the central player in the American political order. That would seem to contradict the intentions of the Founding Fathers. Remembering the horrid example of the British monarchy, they invented a separation of powers in order, as Justice Brandeis later put it, "to preclude the exercise of arbitrary power." Accordingly, they divided the government into three allegedly equal and coordinate branches — the executive, the legislative, and the judiciary.

But a system based on the tripartite separation of powers has an inherent tendency toward inertia and stalemate. One of the three branches must take the initiative if the system is to move. The executive branch alone is structurally capable of taking that initiative. The Founders must have sensed this when they accepted Alexander Hamil-

9

ton's proposition in the Seventieth Federalist that "energy in the executive is a leading character in the definition of good government." They thus envisaged a strong president — but within an equally strong system of constitutional accountability. (The term *imperial presidency* arose in the 1970s to describe the situation when the balance between power and accountability is upset in favor of the executive.)

The American system of self-government thus comes to focus in the presidency — "the vital place of action in the system," as Woodrow Wilson put it. Henry Adams, himself the great-grandson and grandson of presidents as well as the most brilliant of American historians, said that the American president "resembles the commander of a ship at sea. He must have a helm to grasp, a course to steer, a port to seek." The men in the White House (thus far only men, alas) in steering their chosen courses have shaped our destiny as a nation.

Biography offers an easy education in American history, rendering the past more human, more vivid, more intimate, more accessible, more connected to ourselves. Biography reminds us that presidents are not supermen. They are human beings too, worrying about decisions, attending to wives and children, juggling balls in the air, and putting on their pants one leg at a time. Indeed, as Emerson contended, "There is properly no history; only biography."

Presidents serve us as inspirations, and they also serve us as warnings. They provide bad examples as well as good. The nation, the Supreme Court has said, has "no right to expect that it will always have wise and humane rulers, sincerely attached to the principles of the Constitution. Wicked men, ambitious of power, with hatred of liberty and contempt of law, may fill the place once occupied by Washington and Lincoln."

The men in the White House express the ideals and the values, the frailties and the flaws, of the voters who send them there. It is altogether natural that we should want to know more about the virtues and the vices of the fellows we have elected to govern us. As we know more about them, we will know more about ourselves. The French political philosopher Joseph de Maistre said, "Every nation has the government it deserves."

At the start of the twenty-first century, forty-two men have made it to the Oval Office. (George W. Bush is counted our forty-third president, because Grover Cleveland, who served nonconsecutive terms, is counted twice.) Of the parade of presidents, a dozen or so lead the polls periodically conducted by historians and political scientists. What makes a great president?

Great presidents possess, or are possessed by, a vision of an ideal America. Their passion, as they grasp the helm, is to set the ship of state on the right course toward the port they seek. Great presidents also have a deep psychic connection with the needs, anxieties, dreams of people. "I do not believe," said Wilson, "that any man can lead who does not act . . . under the impulse of a profound sympathy with those whom he leads — a sympathy which is insight — an insight which is of the heart rather than of the intellect."

"All of our great presidents," said Franklin D. Roosevelt, "were leaders of thought at a time when certain ideas in the life of the nation had to be clarified." So Washington incarnated the idea of federal union, Jefferson and Jackson the idea of democracy, Lincoln union and freedom, Cleveland rugged honesty. Theodore Roosevelt and Wilson, said FDR, were both "moral leaders, each in his own way and his own time, who used the presidency as a pulpit."

To succeed, presidents not only must have a port to seek but they must convince Congress and the electorate that it is a port worth seeking. Politics in a democracy is ultimately an educational process, an adventure in persuasion and consent. Every president stands in Theodore Roosevelt's bully pulpit.

The greatest presidents in the scholars' rankings, Washington, Lincoln, and Franklin Roosevelt, were leaders who confronted and overcame the republic's greatest crises. Crisis widens presidential opportunities for bold and imaginative action. But it does not guarantee presidential greatness. The crisis of secession did not spur Buchanan or the crisis of depression spur Hoover to creative leadership. Their inadequacies in the face of crisis allowed Lincoln and the second Roosevelt to show the difference individuals make to history. Still, even in the absence of first-order crisis, forceful and persuasive presidents — Jefferson, Jackson, James K. Polk, Theodore Roosevelt, Harry Truman, John F. Kennedy, Ronald Reagan, George W. Bush — are able to impose their own priorities on the country.

The diverse drama of the presidency offers a fascinating set of tales. Biographies of American presidents constitute a chronicle of wisdom and folly, nobility and pettiness, courage and cunning, forthrightness and deceit, quarrel and consensus. The turmoil perennially swirling around the White House illuminates the heart of the American democracy.

It is the aim of the American Presidents series to present the grand panorama of our chief executives in volumes compact enough for the busy reader, lucid enough for the student, authoritative enough for the scholar. Each volume offers a distillation of character and career. I hope that these lives will give readers some understanding of the pitfalls and potentialities of the presidency and also of the responsibilities of citizenship. Truman's famous sign — "The buck stops here" — tells only half the story. Citizens cannot escape the ultimate responsibility. It is in the voting booth, not on the presidential desk, that the buck finally stops.

— Arthur M. Schlesinger, Jr.

INTRODUCTION

Richard Milhous Nixon was an improbable president. He didn't particularly like people. He lacked charm or humor or joy. Socially awkward and an introvert, he had few friends and was virtually incapable of small talk. He didn't care to, in his words, "press the flesh." He was also one of our most complex presidents: insecure, self-pitying, vindictive, suspicious — even literally paranoid — and filled with long-nursed anger and resentments, which burst forth from time to time. He never seemed the happy warrior.

Even reaching the pinnacle of American politics didn't satisfy him. The mixing of his psyche with the presidency made for a poisonous brew, with tragic consequences, as he became the first president to be driven from office. Strikingly, and openly, self-preoccupied, Nixon often talked or wrote about his inner feelings, sometimes with startling self-knowledge. Nixon's first book was titled *Six Crises,* about what he saw as his own ordeals. During his presidency he referred to it often, urging people to read it.

The historian David Greenberg has written that Nixon's unusual personality unleashed "an unprecedented national seminar on the hidden workings of the incumbent president's mind." Even Henry Kissinger, Nixon's national security adviser and later secretary of state, remarked, "Can you imagine what this man would have been if someone loved him?"[1] Nixon was our most Shakespearean president; he brought us into his tragedy and made us go through it with him. He was the second president (but not the last) to face impeachment proceedings, though the proceedings against him were the most serious and least partisan. He was forced to resign his office before the full House of Representatives could vote on the articles of impeachment approved by the House Judiciary Committee, or the Senate could vote to convict him. By that time, he had no choice.

But Nixon was much more than the cartoon figure with the perpetual five o'clock shadow, his arms extended upward, his fingers forming a V. He accomplished a great deal more than is usually granted him

16

— in large part because it's difficult not to view his presidency through the prism of Watergate and impeachment.

He has come to be widely considered our last progressive Republican president, picking up where William McKinley and Theodore Roosevelt left off. But his apparent progressiveness was so mixed with pragmatism and not a little cynicism, and so rooted in the politics of his time, and his interest in domestic policy was so limited, that there is reason to question whether he was a true believer in progressive policies and whether he would have held to them in a later, more conservative, Republican age. Even as he ran for the presidency in 1968, Nixon set in motion the turn of the Republican Party to the right. His foreign policy was marked by highs and lows.

For all his self-pity, Nixon was amazingly resilient to the end, not only surviving his defeats — which were of a magnitude that would have broken other figures — but coming back and back, creating his own restorations, repeatedly presenting the public with a "New Nixon." Yet while he convinced some pundits and others that there really was a "New Nixon," and he maintained a following until nearly the end, he also aroused unusually strong hatred

17

among the American public — a hatred that has lingered long after his death.

How did such a peculiar man become president, and win reelection? In part it was that resilience, and also his fierce and dogged determination. Nixon displayed extraordinary grit; he was unusually willing to do the scut work of politics; he knew the country district by district, doing favors for myriad other politicians, expecting their support in return. Moreover, he was an exceptionally smart man, with a solid command of wide-ranging information, and an able politician. He was a product of his times as well as the pioneer of the rough political tactics for which he became famous — and loathed. Also, in light of what came later, it's important to recall that when Dwight D. Eisenhower selected him as his running mate in 1952, Nixon was a hero to a large swath of the American public, a star of the Republican Party. After that, he benefited from the Republican Party's traditional respect for hierarchy and its tendency to select tested warhorses. And, as in the case of many successful politicians, there was an element of luck in his triumph. Many observers believed that had Lyndon B. Johnson imposed a bombing pause in Vietnam a week earlier than he did at the end of October 1968, Vice President Hubert Humphrey, who was rapidly gaining on Nixon, might well have won that election. He also benefited by the selection in 1972, at a time when the social upheavals caused by the Vietnam War were at a peak, of George McGovern, the favorite of the antiwar left of the Democratic Party, at a raucous convention. McGovern went on to have a string of bad luck himself.

As a journalist in Washington I covered the Nixon presidency, and I wrote a book about the extraordinary period called Watergate. Nixon's tumultuous presidency was for those of us who lived through it the most riveting of our lifetimes and, perhaps, in all of American history. Those who went through that time with him are left with vivid memories: Nixon standing behind the podium at a press conference in the East Room of the White House as the Watergate scandal began to unfold, his hips swiveling as if within a hula hoop; Nixon telling the nation, "I am not a crook"; Nixon playing with a yo-yo on the stage of the Grand Ole Opry; Nixon's tearful farewell speech to his staff. And then the final overhead Vs as he boarded the helicopter to return to California. It has been said that Nixon's was a "criminal presidency," but that misses the larger point. He put the nation through an unprecedented constitutional crisis, during which for a long while it wasn't clear that our system of government would hold. It was a frightening time.

But his presidency was much more as well.

1

Up from Yorba Linda

Richard Nixon had a hard early life. He was born on January 9, 1913, in a seven-hundred-foot frame house his father had built in Yorba Linda, California. The town, set among citrus groves in Orange County, was home to about two hundred people, most of them struggling financially. For many years, the Nixon house had no running water or electricity. Dick Nixon was the second of five sons — two of whom died young — born to Frank and Hannah Milhous Nixon. Frank, born in Ohio of Scots-Irish descent, was quarrelsome and combustible; by all accounts, it was difficult to win his approval, and he thrashed his sons when they crossed him. Hannah, a devout Quaker whose parents had migrated to California from Indiana, came from a middle-class, stable milieu (her parents objected to the marriage). She was selfless toward others but at home was cold, remote, and undemonstrative, and she devoted most of her attention to her two sickly sons. She was also stinting in her praise of her brightest son's achievements. Frank, who had a minimal education, ran away from home when he was thirteen, holding a number of jobs until he moved to California, where he became a streetcar conductor. Hannah, whose family was somewhat better off, attended Whittier College for two years. After their marriage, Frank ran a lemon orchard that failed and worked as a roustabout in an oil field.

When Nixon was nine, the family moved to nearby Whittier, which was composed predominantly of transplanted midwesterners who tended toward conservatism and was dominated by Quakers.[1] The California Quakers were different from their eastern brethren; they weren't necessarily pacifists and were more evangelical and less liberal. The Nixons attended church on Wednesday nights as well as on Sundays.[2] The citizens of Whittier, like those of many southern California towns, believed in temperance, banned public dancing, and closed the cinemas on Sundays.[3] Frank Nixon opened a gasoline station, later expanding it into a grocery store where the entire family worked. Customers steered clear of the volatile Frank, preferring to deal with Hannah. As a teenager, Richard often arose at four a.m. to drive to Los Angeles to buy produce for the store.

Richard Nixon was a precocious child. He taught himself to read before he entered the first grade. He was an A student throughout his education, often finishing near the top of his class. He won oratorical contests, had a phenomenal memory, and was valedictorian of his eighth-grade class. A loner as a child, he preferred to be by himself, talking little, lying in the grass and staring at the sky. Despite his social awkwardness, he was elected several times to leadership positions by his classmates, indicating an early knack for politics — and high ambitions. His early life also suggests a propensity for taking risks, putting himself on the line in order to succeed — in school politics, debating, sports. Despite having a slight build, and no real natural athletic ability, he went out for football. Nixon tried to be "one of the guys," but because of his lack of social skills and his tendency to be a loner, he was more respected than popular in high school.[4]

When Nixon graduated from Whittier High School, his parents lacked the means to send him to an elite college. (He had been offered a scholarship to Harvard but his parents couldn't afford the other expenses of sending him there.) So he was forced to stay home and attend Whittier College. Once again, he went out for football — and was a last-stringer who failed to win a letter. In college, Nixon also led a successful rebellion against the Franklin Club, a group of well-off students who were the powers at the school and had denied him membership; he formed a rival fraternity — the first of his many battles against people of more privilege — and he was elected president of the student body in his senior year. (In that office, he won a battle to introduce dancing at the Quaker college.) During his college years, he steadily dated Ola Florine Welch, a popular and substantive student at Whittier, and they became informally engaged. But it was a stormy relationship; her friends wondered what she saw in Dick Nixon. "He wasn't sexy," one said.[5] She did admire his intellect, but later she dropped him for another man, saying, "Most of the time I just couldn't figure him out."[6] Nixon was stung by the rejection and brooded about it for years.[7]

After graduating from college in 1934, Nixon attended Duke University Law School, a good law school but not considered among the top ones in the country.

Once again, his parents couldn't afford to send him to a more prestigious school. He held down several jobs while attending Duke on a partial scholarship. Nixon wasn't happy in his law school years; he was hard-working, serious, and remote (he never had a date in those three years), and acquired the nickname "Gloomy Gus," though he did get elected to the presidency of the law school bar association for his senior year. A classmate said he was elected out of "genuine respect for his scholarship" rather than because he was better liked than the other candidate. Nixon barely campaigned for the position and was self-effacing after he won it. No one expected him to go on to greater things.[8] He was embittered when prominent Wall Street law firms declined to hire a Duke graduate, favoring those who attended more prestigious law schools. This was just one of Nixon's several disappointments in his life.

Returning to Whittier in 1937, Nixon got a job in a small law firm, one of whose partners had gone to college with Hannah Nixon. His work mainly consisted of probate and real estate cases. Before long Nixon had become a partner in the firm, earning a good salary, but (not unlike his father) he lost a lot of money in a failed frozen orange juice venture. He assumed local leadership roles and became president of the Whittier College Alumni Association.

In 1938, Nixon met Thelma (Pat) Ryan during an appearance by the two of them in a play put on by the Whittier Community Players. Pat, too, had come from harsh circumstances — born in a miner's shack in Nevada. Her mother died at an early age, and Pat took over her duties. She worked her way through college in California, graduated cum laude, and taught commercial classes at Whittier High School. Nixon said it was love at first sight, and he told Pat right away that he was going to marry her. Pat, a spirited redhead, wasn't interested. Nixon pursued her as doggedly as he pursued other goals, even driving her to her dates with other men. After more than two years, she relented, and they were married on June 21, 1940.

According to the author Kati Marton, though the union began as a love match, it was a "misalliance" that led to a "lifeless marriage."[9] Pat thought she was marrying an up-and-coming attorney who would take her far from Whittier. She hated politics. Later the cold and distant Nixon often snubbed her in public. Their two daughters, Tricia and Julie, who were born in 1946 and

1948, respectively, did love their father; Julie was particularly fierce in her support of him as his troubles mounted later.

Though Nixon grew up in California, he was rootless for the rest of his life, and he moved often. He lacked, in Garry Wills's term, the "stamp of place."[10] He had no equivalent of John F. Kennedy's Hyannis Port or Lyndon Johnson's and Ronald Reagan's ranches, or the Bush family's Kennebunkport. As president he took many of his vacations in Key Biscayne, Florida, a haven of the unrooted.

In early 1942, having seized upon an opportunity to get out of Whittier, Nixon took a job in Washington with the Office of Price Administration, for which he had been recommended by a former law school professor. The experience turned him against government controls and the federal bureaucracy. Later that year, when the navy issued a call for lawyers, a bored Nixon volunteered as a lieutenant. Though he served in the Pacific, he never saw combat. During his military service, he spent much of his time reading serious books and was an avid — and successful — poker player. He resigned from the navy in 1945 to run for his first political office.

2

THE RISE AND FALL AND RISE OF RICHARD NIXON

Nixon's political career was one of triumph and failure, sweet victories and bitter losses, a long search for vindication. Throughout his political career, he talked often, even obsessively, about his real and perceived enemies, especially those among the more privileged classes and the elites, and these feelings were blended into his politics. His doggedness was exceptional, even as politicians go. His political ruthlessness made him a reviled figure, but he was in a ruthless profession. Still, his tactics, while not unique or in some cases even original with him, were, for his times, at the outer edges of opportunism and savageness.

The pattern was set in his first political race. He was drafted in 1945 by some local Whittier businessmen to take on the liberal five-term congressman Jerry Voorhis, scion of a wealthy family and a graduate of Yale, in the next election. Nixon, then thirty-two years old, promised the businessmen that he'd "tear Voorhis to pieces."[1] The Nixon–Voorhis race took place in the context of the onset of the Cold War; in 1946, Winston Churchill declared in Fulton, Missouri, that an "iron curtain" had descended across Europe, and FBI director J. Edgar Hoover was warning that communists were infiltrating the federal government and labor unions. Candidates across the country were invoking the "Red Menace."[2]

Portraying himself in his campaign as the "fighting Quaker" and distributing pictures of himself with helmet in hand (though he'd never seen combat), Nixon spoke of "lip-service Americans" and attacked Voorhis as a sympathizer with labor union communists and voting for their interests. Nixon also charged that Moscow was trying to influence voters on Voorhis's behalf.[3] The mid-1940s were an anxious time for other reasons as well; the transition from a wartime to a peacetime economy was taking its toll on several industries, especially the aircraft industry in southern California. Nixon ran as the champion of the "Forgotten Man," a conservative populist, reflecting the antigovernment, anti–big business opinions of much of southern California, as well as his own experience at the Office of Price Administration. To help with his campaign, Nixon hired Murray Chotiner, a lawyer and political operative known as a rough tactician. Chotiner's guiding insight was that people voted against, not for; the key to winning was to put your opponent on the defensive — early.[4] Chotiner would remain at Nixon's side for a long time. Nixon defeated Voorhis soundly, 57 percent to 43 percent.

Upon arriving in Washington in January 1947, Nixon lobbied to retain Voorhis's seat on the House Un-American Activities Committee (HUAC), the perfect setting for continuing his anticommunist crusade — and, as it turned out, to gain national attention. His big break came in August 1948, when Whittaker Chambers, a rumpled, brilliant former communist and now an editor at *Time,* testified before the committee that Alger Hiss, a courtly, wealthy, and well-connected former State Department official and now the president of the prestigious Carnegie Endowment, had been a Soviet agent in the late 1930s. Nixon seized the issue, hauling Hiss in for questioning before the committee and working with Chambers to prove his charge. Hiss denied that he had ever met Chambers, but to the astonishment of most in the circles of which Hiss was a part, Chambers and Nixon later turned out to be right: Hiss was convicted of perjury in 1950 and sent to prison. The Hiss case made Nixon a national anticommunist star, and he campaigned on the issue across the country in 1948. Though he had triumphed in it and by it, Nixon considered the Hiss case his first "crisis," referring to it throughout the rest of his life.[5]

In the course of his House career, Nixon became an ally of the anticommunist crusader Senator Joseph McCarthy of Wisconsin. Nixon, who had led the way, fed McCarthy material for his famous speech in Wheeling, West Virginia, in 1950, in which McCarthy claimed that "I have in my hand a list of 205 . . . members of the Communist Party and who nevertheless are still working and shaping policy in the State Department." (McCarthy could never prove the charge.) According to McCarthy's biographer Thomas C. Reeves, the language McCarthy used in Wheeling was almost identical to that employed by Nixon in a speech on the House floor a few weeks earlier.[6]

After just two terms in the House, Nixon decided to run for an open U.S. Senate seat in 1950, against Representative Helen Gahagan Douglas. In this campaign, he went even further than he had against Voorhis, and acquired the sobriquet "Tricky Dick," which would linger throughout his career. Once again, it's important to see Nixon's Senate race in its context. The year 1950 was the height of the "Red Scare"; shortly after Hiss was convicted in January, Judith Coplon, a former Justice Department official, and Klaus Fuchs, a physicist who had worked on the atomic bomb, were convicted of espionage for the Soviet Union. In June, a war broke out between communist North Korea and South Korea, and in October Mao Zedong's communist forces, which had taken over China the previous year, joined the war on the side of their North Korean allies. Hollywood issued its blacklist, and loyalty oaths were coming into vogue. President Harry Truman approved the development of the hydrogen bomb. Douglas, an actress who had gone to Barnard College, was a strong supporter of the New Deal. Nixon, picking up on a theme used against Douglas by her Democratic opponent in the primary, cited her votes that were the same as those of a left-wing member of Congress from New York, Vito Marcantonio, a member of the American Labor Party. (This theme had actually been initiated in the 1946 race against Voorhis by the newspaper publisher Herb Klein, who later served as Nixon's communications director.) Though the "communist sympathizer" charge was being employed nationwide that year, Nixon's and Chotiner's innovation was to hand out material about the number of times, which was exaggerated, that Douglas and Marcantonio had voted together on a pink flyer.[7] Douglas became tarred as the "Pink Lady." Nixon also attacked Douglas as an eastern elitist, contrasting her with himself as a family man of modest means; he also made thinly veiled references to the Jewish origins of her husband, the actor Melvyn Douglas. Whittaker Chambers's biographer Sam Tanenhaus has speculated that Nixon didn't need the anticommunist smear to defeat Douglas; not only were the issues on Nixon's side, but also he was the far better politician.[8] Nixon was widely considered an attractive figure; newspapers described him as "tall, dark and handsome." Nixon won with 59 percent of the vote. If Nixon was ruthless in his 1950 election, he was also in fashion. In the Florida Democratic primary in that same election year, Congressman George Smathers defeated the incumbent senator Claude Pepper by branding him "Red Pepper." Maryland Democratic senator Millard Tydings was defeated on similar charges, with his opponent brandishing a cropped picture purporting to show Tydings with Earl Browder, the head of the Communist Party in America, and Joseph McCarthy and his allies also took credit for the defeat of Illinois senator and majority leader Scott Lukas by Everett McKinley Dirksen. But it was Nixon's tactics — and the nickname they earned him — that stood out.

Now a genuine national figure and hero to many in the Republican Party, after two years in the Senate, a bored and restless Nixon was ready to move up. With the help of Chotiner and some California businessmen, Nixon maneuvered strenuously, and deviously, for a place on the party's presidential ticket in 1952. California governor Earl Warren was a dark-horse candidate in the race for the nomination between Ohio senator Robert Taft, a conservative isolationist and stiff campaigner, and the World War II hero Dwight Eisenhower, who was especially popular with the business and internationalist wings of the Republican Party, and Warren was the de facto head of the California delegation to the Republican National Convention. But a group of California businessmen (who found Warren too progressive) enlisted a very willing Nixon to swing the delegation to Eisenhower. It was obvious to Nixon that his best opportunity for political advancement lay with the popular general. So with his characteristic combination of political and dark genius, Nixon pretended to the Taft forces that he was for their man — in order to secure his own right flank and to lead Taft to believe that he needn't campaign much in California — and began to work against Warren, first by giving tepid speeches about him while praising Eisenhower's broad appeal, and then by agreeing to sign a pledge to be a loyal supporter of Warren only after extracting a promise that he would be allowed to select nearly half of the California delegates.

While he was NATO commander, Eisenhower had met Nixon briefly in Paris and was pleased that the grave young politician shared his views as an internationalist; and Nixon had the good sense not to talk to Eisenhower about American politics at a time when the general was being implored to run for president. Eisenhower prided himself on not joining in on the red-baiting demagogy of the times, and was somehow under the impression that Nixon was of the same view. But, unfamiliar as he was with American politics, Eisenhower essentially left the selection of his running mate to his own political advisers. They were impressed with Nixon as an up-and-coming politician, and with the electoral importance of California, and they dangled the slot of running mate to Nixon two months before the nominating convention. At Chotiner's suggestion, Nixon joined the California delegation on the train journey to Chicago, where the convention was to begin on July 7, and excitedly spread the false information that Taft was losing ground to Eisenhower. At the same time he pledged his complete loyalty directly to Warren, who was also on the train, and then proceeded through the cars telling the delegates that Warren had no chance to win and that they should throw their support to Eisenhower. Chotiner, who had put himself in charge of convention logistics, pulled such stunts as switching the banners on the delegation's buses from ones for Warren to ones proclaiming "Eisenhower for President." In the end, of course, Eisenhower won the nomination and then "chose" the running mate that had been selected by his advisers. Upon receiving word that Eisenhower had chosen him, Nixon burst into Eisenhower's suite, saying, "Congratulations, Chief" — an informal parlance that clearly caused Eisenhower to bristle.[9] Their relationship was not off to a great start.

In the fall campaign, Eisenhower stood above the fray, refusing to be drawn into harsh partisan attacks or red-baiting, while Nixon, a natural, did the dirty work. He drew on a deep vein in American politics: anti-intellectualism. He called the Democratic candidate, Governor Adlai Stevenson of Illinois, "Adlai the Appeaser . . . who got a Ph.D. degree from Acheson's College of Cowardly Containment"[10] — a reference to Secretary of State Dean Acheson, who was widely reviled in Republican circles. He went after Truman and the Democrats with particular partisan zeal and harshness; he called Stevenson "Mr. Truman's stooge" without "backbone training"; and continuing his red-baiting, he referred to "a godless, ruthless, atheistic, and sinister foe that has infiltrated some of our key institutions."[11]

Then came a potentially catastrophic political crisis — the revelation in September 1952 that Nixon had been the beneficiary of a "secret fund" established by some wealthy backers, most of them Californians, to help cover his political expenses. Though the slush fund was neither illegal at the time nor unique, its exposure caused an uproar and put his place on the Republican ticket in doubt, as one of Eisenhower's campaign themes was to clean up the "mess in Washington" — referring to the corruption charges that had been brought against the Truman administration. Eisenhower at first did not respond to the allegations about the fund, leaving Nixon in a precarious spot. While Eisenhower hesitated to come to Nixon's defense, Nixon exploded to him in one conversation, "There comes a time on matters like these when you've either got to shit or get off the pot."[12] The comment didn't endear him to Eisenhower, a dignified man not accustomed to being spoken to in that way.

While his fate was in question, Nixon decided he had to defend himself publicly. With Eisenhower's approval, on September 23 he went on national television to deliver a thirty-minute address. Eisenhower actually sent word to Nixon indirectly (as was his style) that he should offer his resignation at the end of the speech — leaving Eisenhower to accept it or keep Nixon on if his speech received a strong popular response — but Nixon ignored the request.[13] In the speech, Nixon presented himself as a plainspoken man of modest financial means, once again identifying himself with the common man, and avoided addressing the issue of the fund itself. The most famous part of the speech was Nixon's diversionary tactic of referring to his wife's "respectable cloth coat" (as opposed to the mink coats the Democratic administration had been charged with accepting) and, irrelevantly, talked about a cocker spaniel named Checkers that his daughters had been given by some supporters. "Regardless of what they say about it, we're gonna keep it," he insisted.

To bring pressure on Eisenhower, Nixon asked viewers to send telegrams of support to the Republican National Committee, and the outpouring was enormous. Despite its controversial nature, what has gone down in history as the "Checkers speech" went over well with a wide swath of the American public. After delaying for a while longer — concerned about the fact that Nixon hadn't come clean about the fund — and keeping Nixon in suspense, Eisenhower, understanding that if Nixon were dropped from the ticket his own candidacy might be doomed, finally told Nixon, "You're my boy," and kept him as his running mate. But Eisenhower and Nixon would never trust each other again.[14] Nixon wrote in *Six Crises,* "I felt now that it was my battle alone. I had been deserted by so many I had thought were friends."[15] Apparently, Pat Nixon never got over this event, which deepened her disdain for politics; in fact, she persuaded her husband to write her a pledge that after this campaign he would abandon politics.[16] That pledge would soon be forgotten.

The Eisenhower–Nixon ticket won handily in November 1952. After they were elected, Eisenhower used Nixon to rein in McCarthy — whom by then Nixon considered so inept as to have damaged the anticommunist cause. Like most of his predecessors, he represented the president on numerous foreign trips. (On a trip to South America during his second term, he was spat upon by young anti-American protesters and mobs pelted his limousine with rocks and clubs. This incident was to earn another chapter in *Six Crises*.) Yet his relationship with President Eisenhower was distant — Nixon would later complain that he had never been invited into Eisenhower's house in Gettysburg, Pennsylvania. In 1956, Nixon survived another effort to drop him from the ticket, as moderates and other opponents joined in a "Dump Nixon" movement, and even Eisenhower had doubts, feeling that Nixon "just hadn't grown" and needed other executive experience.[17] But Nixon had already created the first "New Nixon," setting aside his rough campaign tactics and presenting himself as a thoughtful, reasonable man, and so he stayed on the ticket, and his eight years as next in line to the popular Eisenhower put him in a commanding position to win the Republican presidential nomination in 1960.

Nixon won the nomination with little opposition. New York governor Nelson Rockefeller had prepared to challenge Nixon but once it was clear that he aroused little public support and that Nixon had the nomination all but sewn up, he bowed out before a single primary was held. But Nixon wasn't so sure that Rockefeller would simply stand by, and in fact the New York governor went through spates of wooing delegates, so on the eve of the convention, Nixon decided that he could win the nomination by courting the party's more liberal wing and he flew to New York to meet with Rockefeller and adopt what became known as the "Compact of Fifth Avenue," a fourteen-point program dictated by Rockefeller, pledging to call for an increase in national defense spending and enforcement of civil rights.[18]

The opponent for the general election

Nixon feared most was Massachusetts senator John F. Kennedy. While Kennedy and Nixon enjoyed a cordial relationship in the Senate, Kennedy represented everything Nixon envied and resented — privilege, wealth, charm, charisma, and prominent connections. Nixon was advised not to debate the lesser-known Kennedy, but he relished confrontations, had confidence from earlier debate victories, and couldn't resist. The first of their four debates that fall went to Kennedy among the television viewers on poise and cool; Nixon, famously, was badly made up and perspiring, wearing a gray suit that blended with the walls. (Television was a relatively new medium then.) But Nixon won on substance among those who listened to it on the radio. Still, Kennedy came off as more the statesman, more positive than Nixon, whose sharp criticism of Kennedy — at the same time that Kennedy was addressing the public on larger issues — reminded people why Nixon was so widely disliked. Kennedy charged that the Eisenhower administration had allowed a "missile gap" to develop between the United States and the Soviet Union (later, his secretary of defense, Robert McNamara, revealed that there was no such gap), and emphasized the communist take-over of Cuba by Fidel Castro and his support of civil rights.

As the race went on, Nixon became increasingly tense and wound up. His loss to Kennedy in the popular vote was narrow — by just 118,574 votes out of 68,837,000 cast — but the electoral vote victory for Kennedy of 303–219 was crushing.[19] Many Nixon supporters claimed that the Kennedy family had stolen the election, particularly in Illinois. But even if the machine of Chicago mayor Richard M. Daley did steal Illinois, Kennedy still would have won the electoral college without it.[20] Though others urged Nixon to challenge the outcome, he declined to do so. This reflected not so much unusual magnanimity as a recognition of reality: Republican National Committee chairman Thruston Morton urged local party officials to take legal action "on the alleged vote fraud" in eleven states, but no significant fraud was found.[21]

A great many of Nixon's opponents assumed that his loss in 1960 was the end of his political career, but this was another underestimation of the man's remarkable resilience and grit. He returned to California, practiced law, and, at Kennedy's suggestion, went to work on a political memoir, which became *Six Crises.*[22] But Nixon had no intention of dropping out of politics, and at the invitation of some state Republicans he ran for governor in 1962, challenging the incumbent, Edmund G. "Pat" Brown; Nixon saw the California governorship as a way station en route to the presidency. He survived a close primary, in which a candidate who was to his right charged him with being an opportunist and not a true believer in the conservative cause. Damaged by the primary and distrusted by a large number of Californians (who also remembered his betrayal of Earl Warren), Nixon was defeated by Brown 52 percent to 47 percent. The most famous moment of the race came after it was over, in what Nixon called his "last press conference." Tired and angry, he told the press, "You don't have Nixon to kick around anymore." Many thought, again, that this was the end of Nixon's political career.

Following his loss in California, Nixon moved to New York and joined a prominent law firm there. In 1966, he came out of political exile to campaign extensively for Republican candidates for Congress, piling up the IOUs. The following January, he began planning his next race for the presidency.[23]

The 1968 election would finally bring Nixon the political triumph he had long sought. The election was fought against the backdrop of the most turbulent years of the 1960s — marked by violent urban riots, apparent setbacks for U.S. forces in Vietnam, the rise of the largest antiwar movement in the nation's history, increasingly angry protests by civil rights groups, campus uproar, and social upheavals. The "hippies" of the 1960s abandoned middle-class values and rejected authority — and received a great deal of television coverage. Blacks were turning away from their more moderate leaders like Martin Luther King Jr. and beginning to follow more militant ones, such as Stokely Carmichael, the leader of the new Black Power movement. The enactment of the Civil Rights Act of 1964 and the Voting Rights Act of 1965 had stirred deep resentment among southern whites.

At that time, President Lyndon Johnson was a prisoner in his own country. He was under political siege from antiwar candidate Eugene McCarthy, who nearly defeated him in the New Hampshire primary, and Robert F. Kennedy, who entered the race after McCarthy's strong showing. On March 31, Johnson made his stunning announcement (even to most of his own staff) that he wouldn't seek his party's renomination, throwing open the race for the presidency. This created an opening for his vice president, Hubert Humphrey. Later that week, racial turmoil exploded following the murder of King in Memphis. The assassination of Robert Kennedy, on the night of his California primary victory in the early hours of June 5, added trauma upon trauma — and effectively ended the race for the nomination. The 1968 Democratic National Convention in Chicago was characterized by antiwar demonstrations, the beating up of demonstrators by Mayor Daley's police, and a raucous convention hall. Though Humphrey won the nomination, a great many of the delegates' hearts remained with McCarthy and Kennedy, and a large number of Democrats were never reconciled to Humphrey. It was the perfect setting for backlash politics.

Nixon appealed to the great number of Americans who resented and feared the cultural and social upheavals of the time. He stood with them against liberals, the East Coast, intellectuals, big government, and racial minorities. He spoke for, he said, "the silent majority" — a term that would recur later in his political career. Garry Wills wrote in *Nixon Agonistes,* "If a politics of resentment was taking shape in 1968, no one knew that fact better than the man who would, at each stage of that year, prove himself the master of the situation."[24]

The idea was to put together a new coalition, consisting of blue-collar workers who, particularly as a result of Franklin D. Roosevelt's New Deal, had been voting for Democrats for economic reasons, and of southerners who had voted Democratic for nearly a century following the Civil War — both groups angered by essentially the same things: the civil rights revolution, which embraced integration and school busing, and student radicals, hippies, and other antiwar demonstrators, which they associated with liberals, who were also associated with an ever larger and more intrusive federal government. A major component of Nixon's effort was the "Southern Strategy." When Lyndon Johnson signed the 1964 civil rights bill, he said, presciently, "There goes the South."[25] Barry Goldwater, the Republican nominee in 1964, had won five southern states by opposing the passage of the Civil Rights Act of 1964 and denouncing centralized government, and Nixon picked up where Goldwater had left off. With anticommunism no longer the effective issue it had been in the 1940s and '50s,

Nixon also campaigned on the theme of "law and order," which Goldwater had emphasized, as a way to appeal to southern segregationists and the white working class of the north. While Nixon was seeking the nomination, he had promised the segregationist senator Strom Thurmond of South Carolina that he would respect the views of southerners on the matter of the courts, and told southern delegates at the Republican Convention in Miami that he would not support "some professional civil rights group."[26] His first big gesture toward the South was his surprise selection of the governor of Maryland, Spiro Agnew, a little-known mediocrity, as his running mate. (One of the few things that Agnew was known for was that he had sternly lectured black leaders after some riots in Baltimore.) Nixon would leave most of the campaign's dirty work to Agnew, leading some journalists to write glowingly, not for the first or last time, about the "New Nixon," who stood above the fray.

Thus, in the course of the 1968 campaign, Nixon effected the first great realignment of American politics since Franklin Roosevelt in 1932. He created what his campaign strategist Kevin Phillips described in his important 1969 book, *The Emerging Repub-*

lican Majority, as a coalition of the South, the mountain states, California, and blue-collar workers of the North — against a minority Democratic Party based in the Northeast and the Pacific Northwest.[27] During the Republican primaries, Nixon announced his strategy in a speech in May and a pamphlet called "A New Alignment for American Unity." As Garry Wills pointed out, Nixon talked in terms of "alignment," not consensus. In fact, Nixon said explicitly, "We will not seek the false unity of consensus, of the glossing over of fundamental differences." Wills observed that the common note among the groups Nixon chose to put together was "resentment of government."[28] Nixon attacked the "liberal" Supreme Court, promised to reduce taxes and increase defense spending, and criticized the expansion of the federal government's role through Lyndon Johnson's "Great Society."[29] Nixon was aided in 1968 not only by the deep divisions in the Democratic Party, but also by the independent candidacy of Alabama governor George Wallace, a segregationist populist who ran against "forced busing" and "pointy-headed intellectuals," and who also sought to take votes away from the Democrats.

For his part, Hubert Humphrey chose to

remain loyal to President Johnson, to whom he was indebted, thus trapping himself in Johnson's Vietnam policy. Only toward the end of the campaign did Humphrey begin to put some distance between himself and Johnson, calling for a pause in the bombing of North Vietnam. Meanwhile Nixon, who had answered in the affirmative, though dishonestly, when a reporter asked him if he had a "secret plan" to end the war, meddled with the peace talks taking place in Paris.

On October 31, Johnson announced an agreement to halt the bombing of North Vietnam; the South Vietnamese government two days later rejected the agreement. The bombing halt ordered by Johnson came too late to help Humphrey. He was gaining momentum in the days before the election, but Nixon won with 43.4 percent of the vote to Humphrey's 42.7 and Wallace's 13.5. (Forty percent of Wallace's vote came from outside the South.) Nixon had transformed the party of Abraham Lincoln into the party that welcomed racists and despisers of big government, setting in motion a Republican conservative ascendancy.

3
GOVERNING STYLE

President-elect Richard Nixon was surprisingly unprepared for the presidency. The transition from Lyndon Johnson to Richard Nixon was marked by striking indecision and delays. It was the start of a curiously indecisive presidency. When he was elected president, Nixon had no idea who he wanted in his cabinet, or what he wanted to do once in office. His eight years' experience as vice president did little to offset the inexperience of those he brought in to serve him in the White House — most of them chosen for their pugnacity and proven loyalty, rather than for their substantive knowledge or interest in policy.

As the journalists Rowland Evans and Robert Novak wrote of the vice-presidential years, "Surrounded by enemies bent on his destruction, Nixon had little time for self-education."[1] Eisenhower had essentially shut him out. (When Lyndon and Lady

51

Bird Johnson showed the Nixons the second-floor, residential part of the White House, it appeared that this was the first time they had seen it.)[2] Nixon's career on Capitol Hill had been brief — he had spent only four years in the House and two in the Senate — and had been dominated by his anticommunist crusade and his commitment to his own political ascent. So Nixon came to the transition with few substantive plans for his administration. He had campaigned principally on "law and order," and, though he mentioned some domestic programs in his radio addresses, Nixon didn't see these programs as the basis for governing, and his staff didn't take them seriously. Evans and Novak observed that Nixon brought to his transition "very little" in the way of substantive ideas: "On the economy, the environment and civil rights, there was a total absence of planning," and that "his initial ideas about tax incentives to take the place of social-welfare plans fell apart when they were closely examined."[3] In fact, Nixon was little interested in domestic policy; his passion was foreign policy, about which he knew a great deal. And though he had a very quick and analytical mind, he was uncomfortable concentrating on two or three large issues at the same time.[4]

Having given the matter little thought, Nixon selected his cabinet in a higgledy-piggledy fashion. The result was, according to Evans and Novak, "perhaps the least distinguished in the postwar era," and it "proved to be precisely the ill-assorted, themeless band that it had seemed at the time of its haphazard selection."[5] The haphazardness also stemmed from the fact that Nixon, under criticism for moving slowly, adopted an artificial deadline to complete the job. Several people turned him down, or made sure that they weren't asked. After he was twice rebuffed by prospective candidates for the post of secretary of state, Nixon turned to his old friend William P. Rogers, a genial, wealthy attorney from a white-shoe firm in New York who had served as attorney general in Eisenhower's second term. Nixon and Rogers had once been close and Nixon had relied on him for advice at crucial times, but the two men had largely gone their separate ways in recent years. Rogers had almost no experience in foreign policy — and was soon to be overrun by the national security adviser, Henry Kissinger. Robert Finch, a Nixon protégé from California politics who had run his 1960 presidential campaign, was chosen to be secretary of health, education, and welfare. Finch was more liberal than many of his colleagues — he quarreled with the conservatives at the White House and the Justice Department over school desegregation — and he also cultivated the press, which was not appreciated by the White House. (In 1970, an exhausted Finch was pushed out of his job and made a White House counselor.) Nixon persuaded Melvin Laird, a shrewd, powerful Republican congressman from Wisconsin, to be his secretary of defense. At least one cabinet choice, George Shultz, whom Nixon selected as secretary of labor, did not fit the norm: Shultz, an economist who had attended Princeton, was the only representative of the Ivy League. In fact, Nixon's original cabinet broke the postwar record with the fewest number of Ivy Leaguers.[6] For the Treasury Department, Nixon chose David Kennedy, a Chicago banker, but Kennedy didn't play a large role in the administration and in 1972 was replaced by the former Texas governor (and former Democrat) John Connally, who in turn would be replaced by George Shultz, followed by William Simon. Nixon didn't really know his "choices" for secretary of the interior (Walter Hickel) or secretary of housing and urban development (George Romney). The one appointment Nixon insisted upon was the selection of his campaign manager and law partner, John Mitchell, as attorney general. Mitchell gave off the aura of wisdom by puffing on a pipe and saying little. It was a fateful appointment. As a public relations gimmick, Nixon presented all of his cabinet appointees at once on a televised appearance on December 11, 1968, declaring his choices to be people of "extra dimension."[7]

Nixon's style of governing was peculiar, and so was the way his White House functioned. On occasion Nixon would issue a barrage of orders — some of which he didn't intend to be carried out but he made for effect. The job of his top aides was to figure out which ones those were — to protect the president from himself. They knew better than to disagree with him openly when he issued a misguided order. When he was agitated, Nixon would make a series of phone calls, barking out an order and then slamming down the phone. A single aide could receive three or more such calls in quick succession, including one where Nixon would bark, "This order is not appealable." Slam. Or: "Anyone who dissents will be fired." Slam.[8] In 1972, as Nixon's reelection approached, White House counsel John Dean ordered the Internal Revenue Service to investigate 490 McGovern staff members and contributors. When Treasury Secretary Shultz objected, Nixon erupted in anger: "If [Shultz] doesn't do it, he's going to be out as secretary of the treasury and that's the way it's going to be played."

Though his top White House aides — chief of staff H. R. Haldeman, chief domestic adviser John Ehrlichman, and Henry Kissinger — knew not to execute some of Nixon's wildest and most dangerous orders, they carried out some that ended up destroying Nixon. And his combative aide Charles (Chuck) Colson, a counselor to the president, wouldn't consider not carrying out Nixon's orders. One problem his aides had was that Nixon, who liked martinis, scotch, and wine, didn't hold liquor well. His words were often slurred after he'd had a few drinks, and he could be at his most pugnacious then. Though his drink of preference was martinis, Nixon knew fine wines and collected them; at dinners, waiters served him those wines, keeping the labels hidden behind a napkin, while his guests were served wine of a lower quality.[9] During Nixon's vice presidency, Eisenhower was sufficiently concerned about his drinking habits that he sent his brother Milton to keep an eye on Nixon when he went to Moscow in 1959 to attend a trade fair, where he participated in his famous "kitchen debate" with Nikita Khrushchev. Milton Eisenhower reported that before one Moscow dinner a nervous Nixon drank "about six martinis" and became quite vulgar.[10] Ehrlichman had been worried ever since he observed Nixon's inebriated behavior at a party the evening following his speech to the 1964 Republican Convention in San Francisco, and thought that Nixon's predilection for drink — and his easy lapses into drunkenness — would prevent his reentry into public life; Ehrlichman warned Nixon that he wouldn't work for him further unless he cut back.[11]

There is strong evidence that Nixon's slurring of words may also have been caused by his use of Dilantin, an anticonvulsive prescription drug that he was self-medicating as an antianxiety agent; Dilantin's side effects include slurred speech, mental confusion, and irritability.[12] Mixed with alcohol, it enhances alcohol's effects. (Dilantin was never approved as a psychiatric drug.) The medicine was first provided to Nixon in 1968 by Jack Dreyfus, a founder of the Dreyfus Fund and a strenuous promoter of the drug. Dreyfus strongly believed that it had helped him through a long and serious depression after his mother died.[13] A very wealthy man and a contributor to both Nixon and Humphrey in 1968 so as to have access to the next president, Dreyfus seemed to have a particular affinity toward Nixon. Dreyfus had already offered him a lucrative job in his company; Nixon turned the offer down, saying that he wanted to stay in politics. But the two men particularly hit it off at a dinner in Miami, arranged by Nixon's friend Bebe Rebozo, in 1968, and they enjoyed a warm relationship throughout the rest of Nixon's life.[14] It was as a result of that dinner that Dreyfus gave Nixon the Dilantin. The information that Nixon used Dilantin first surfaced in Anthony Summers's book *The Arrogance of Power* and was based on the author's interview with Dreyfus; Dreyfus later confirmed this information to the *New York Times.* In an account by Adam Clymer in the *Times* shortly after the book appeared in 2000, Dreyfus said that he gave Nixon one thousand one-hundred-milligram pills in 1968, "when his mood wasn't too good," and that later Nixon asked him for another one thousand pills. Dreyfus also told Clymer that when he suggested that Nixon get a prescription for the medication, Nixon replied, "To heck with the doctor."[15] A striking example of Nixon's slurring of words and seeming out of control was to occur in the days leading up to his reckless invasion of Cambodia.

Most evenings when Nixon was in Washington, he sat alone in the Lincoln Sitting Room in the White House residence, air-conditioning on high, a fire blazing in the fireplace, listening to the sound track of the television documentary *Victory at Sea*. By day he often secreted himself for hours in a hideaway in the Executive Office Building, next to the White House. He spent a great deal of his time writing notes to himself on a yellow legal pad: instructions to aides and also comments demonstrating his self-absorption and determination to shape his own image. In January 1970, he wrote to himself: "Add element of lift to each appearance. . . . Hard work — Imagination — Compassion — Leadership — Understanding of young — Intellectual expansion." He also wrote that day, "Cool — Strong — Organized — Temperat e — Exciting. . . . Excitement — Joy in Life — Sharing. Lift spirit of people — Pithy, memorable phrases."[16]

He immersed himself in details, including

the White House decor, or orders to the White House gardeners and butlers. He checked the seating charts for formal White House dinners, sometimes rearranging them. Nixon preferred soothing, popular classics, both in private and as entertainment for the dinners, because he believed audiences would appreciate that more than contemporary numbers. One aide described Nixon as "aggressively square," but he was in step with most of the public in rejecting the "Woodstock Nation." Nixon also tried to see to it that White House entertainers were Republicans. He did, however, appreciate the popularity of Elvis Presley (no Woodstocker, no Janis Joplin), who unexpectedly turned up at the White House seeking a meeting with Nixon to discuss the drug culture and similar topics. The two men met — a famously photographed event — in December 1970.

Nixon had a ferocious temper and often engaged in threats and tantrums as well as sudden mood swings. His aides did their best to cover this up. According to the author Richard Reeves, "Nixon was angry many days and repetitive most days, saying the same things, usually about firing bureaucrats and cutting off reporters."[17] In fact, the evidence is that by the time Nixon reached the White House, he had developed symptoms of paranoid personality; his behavior met the criteria defined in the official psychiatric diagnostic manual.[18] According to that definition, a paranoid personality doesn't always have the capability of rationally considering ideas. Further, that person's suspiciousness can lead to an inability to confide in others — a clear aspect of Nixon — because of an "unwarranted fear that the information will be used against him." Politics is normally riddled with grudges and jealousies and suspicion, but Nixon's behavior went beyond the normal range. And now, as president, he had the power to act on his paranoia, and he did so — to a degree that was ultimately self-destructive. There were early omens of the crisis that would destroy his presidency.

As the world learned later, Nixon also indulged in unusually foul language and anti-Semitic statements. He talked about the "fucking Jews," and referred to Kissinger, when Kissinger wasn't in the room, as "my Jew-boy."[19] When Elvis Presley offered to help stop the use of marijuana, Nixon replied, "All the Jews seem to be the ones that are for liberalizing the regulations on marijuana."[20]

In 1969, Nixon initiated Sunday prayer

services in the White House.

Some of Nixon's close aides thought that he was several people: polite and generous; thoughtful and impetuous; capable of exercising some progressive instincts; a hating, vindictive, crude man. He needed, and sought, a great deal of flattery; his rages caused his aides to cower and hope that they would blow over. If a staff member did try to challenge his prejudices or dark side, Nixon would cut that person off.[21] This explains a lot of what happened later in his presidency.

Indecisive as he often was, Nixon could also make big and sometimes courageous decisions on foreign policy (he prided himself on this) but it was, Henry Kissinger later said, "a joyless, desperate courage, affected by his fatalistic instinct that nothing he touched would ever be crowned with success."[22]

John Ehrlichman wrote in his memoir, "Nixon liked foreign affairs better. Domestic controversy involved the unsolvable, passion-laden issues no one could enjoy grappling with, and the damnable special-interest groups who always demand and demand more but never show gratitude." Nixon liked the pomp as well as the substance of foreign policy. Ehrlichman said, "Foreign-policy activities — ambassadors ceremonially presenting their credentials, or the exchange of toasts at a summit conference with the Russians — all massage a president's ego," whereas a visit to a sewage plant "didn't make Nixon feel like the leader of the Free World." (He also pointed out that Nixon *did* make such trips.)[23] With his penchant for pomp, in 1970 Nixon put his own personal stamp on how the White House was presented: White House guards were dressed up in comic-opera, Graustarkian costumes: tunics, gold epaulets, and tall hats. Amid the public laughter, the uniforms were retired. In another Nixonian innovation, smartly uniformed trumpeters, their medieval horns dressed in heraldry, announced the approach of the chief executive.[24]

The incoming administration engaged in the standard rhetoric about downgrading the power of the White House staff while it clearly was assembling the largest and potentially most powerful presidential staff in history; the newly named White House officials talked with their predecessors about how to make the cabinet departments more responsive to the White House.[25] Though

63

they also insisted that there would be no all-powerful White House assistant, specifically such as Joseph Califano had been in the Johnson White House, when the departing Califano met with the incoming domestic staff, the new one was already twice the size of his own.[26] But before long one aide emerged as firmly in control: H. R. (Bob) Haldeman, the buzz-cut, cold-blooded former advertising agent and advance man in Nixon's 1968 campaign. The next most powerful aide was John Ehrlichman, a Seattle lawyer and also a former advance man, and a close friend of Haldeman; after the first few months, Ehrlichman was put in charge of domestic policy and in time his staff numbered a staggering eighty people. The dominance of former campaign functionaries led Nixon's White House to focus on politics and process rather than policy. And despite its pledge to "clean house" of Johnson appointees throughout the government, a great many Johnson people held on to their jobs. They continued to serve because they believed in what they were doing.

In fact, the Nixon White House staff was notable for the number of aides under the age of thirty — more than in all previous White House staffs combined.[27] The Nixon presidency paid a price for this. Most of the young aides were technicians drawn from the campaign staff. But a few were young scholars selected by the White House adviser on domestic policy, Daniel Patrick Moynihan, a Harvard professor, member of Kennedy's Labor Department, and an intellectual gadfly. Moynihan and Kissinger were the two intellectual heavyweights in the Nixon White House, one having more effect than the other. Kissinger quickly assembled his staff and proceeded to dominate the formulation and execution of foreign policy.[28]

According to Christopher DeMuth, at the time a twenty-one-year-old Harvard graduate and a member of Moynihan's staff (who later became president of the conservative American Enterprise Institute), in the Nixon White House "the staff was not staff — we were line operators: we felt that the people around the president *were* the government." He added, "I think a Rubicon was passed very early in the administration and the staff got the idea that the White House was an operating agency, not a staff — it was actually executing things — and then we'd inform the cabinet officers." He explained that this was a big factor in Nixon's later downfall, saying, "We felt that if we could operate HUD, we could operate the IRS." He continued, "There were young people there with very bad judgment and too much authority. I think it was a large part of what led to Watergate."[29]

Nixon frequently reorganized his White House staff, but it never really ran smoothly.[30] Arthur M. Schlesinger Jr. wrote in *The Imperial Presidency* that the concentration of power in the Nixon White House "enfeebled the cabinet," and that in Nixon's second term, his cabinet was composed "with one or two exceptions, of clerks, of compliant and faceless men who stood for nothing."[31] He also pointed out that such a concentration of power shielded Nixon's policy process behind executive secrecy, because White House aides could not be called before Congress. Schlesinger quoted the words of Woodrow Wilson's biographer Arthur Link: "The less secure a president is, the larger staff he will want."[32] Also in his second term, Nixon had a preference for "czars" — for energy, for economic policy — who straddled cabinet departments.[33]

Nixon was generally aloof from his staff and preferred that all of them but Haldeman, Ehrlichman, and Kissinger communicate with him by memo, rather than face-to-face.[34] Haldeman and Ehrlichman guarded access to Nixon to such an extent that they came to be called the "Berlin Wall"; few cabinet officers had access to the president. Nixon also hated to deal with confrontations among his advisers, so much so that, to his own disadvantage, he avoided meetings in which policy disagreements could be aired. When he did see his favored aides, Nixon tended to engage in rambling conversations about history, of which he had read a great deal, and about past leaders, and about his own aspirations to great leadership. Ehrlichman wrote, "Access to Nixon had disadvantages too — countless hours of his rambling and rumination."[35]

Nixon also preferred to talk to people on the phone than to see them in person; he often made late-night calls to supporters and staff. While Johnson had had a phone with direct lines to sixty people, Nixon's phone connected him directly with only three people: Haldeman, Ehrlichman, and Kissinger. Only those three, plus his personal secretary, Rose Mary Woods, had "walk-in rights" to the Oval Office.

Nixon even wrote memos to his wife: "To Mrs. Nixon, from The President." The author Kati Marton observed that Nixon's was "a presidency where the chief executive and the first lady lived virtually separate lives."[36] Pat Nixon concentrated on refurbishing the White House. Supportive of her husband in public, she remained unhappy with politics. And though she was privately spirited, she acquired the public image of "Plastic Pat" — the perfect, dutiful, quiet wife. She also undertook a great deal of foreign travel on her own, where her natural, more lively side emerged. Inevitably, there were deep tensions between the first lady and Nixon's palace guard.[37] Though Nixon cared for his daughters, and was especially close to Julie, while he was in the White House he had little time for his family. Nixon would have the staff meet with his daughters to deliver awkward messages.[38]

Nixon spent about 70 percent of his time with Haldeman, though the two men never became intimates.[39] Nixon grew increasingly dependent on his top aide, who was the only person Nixon felt he could talk to — more than his own family or anyone else. Nixon of course had no idea that Haldeman was keeping a meticulous diary, to be published after the chief of staff's death years later, in which one can only believe that Haldeman was unintentionally revealing about the inner workings of the White House and his conversations with the president. (Haldeman also carried around a small camera to record major events.) Haldeman was involved in major policy decisions as well as in trying to keep the White House running smoothly. He worked seven days a week, and often long evenings; he was always available to Nixon, but it appeared that he was more devoted to the Office of the Presidency than to Nixon himself. Nixon called Haldeman his "gatekeeper" — it was Haldeman who said no to all sorts of people, including the vice president and cabinet members, who wanted to see the president. In 1971, Nixon told his cabinet, "Haldeman is the lord high executioner," adding, "Don't you come whining to me when he tells you to do something." Haldeman was willingly Nixon's SOB; he was not known for grace or humanity.[40]

Nixon's taste in movies was revealing and appeared to affect his governing. He watched the movie *Patton* at least five times, sometimes ordering aides to watch it with him; he particularly admired General George S. Patton as a man of boldness and ruthlessness, memorably played by George C. Scott.[41] At Haldeman's suggestion, Nixon began wearing small flag pins in his lapels, and ordered his staff to do the same.[42] Thus, Nixon tried to appropriate patriotism; the flag pins were one of Nixon's legacies.

The White House staff was unusually thorough in blending politics and policy. Members of Congress said that conversations with Nixon about policy invariably turned to his saying, "Now let's talk about the politics of this thing. . . . How it will translate into votes." Ehrlichman was wont to ask of a proposed action, "How will it play in Peoria?" And Attorney General John Mitchell was known to scrutinize virtually all of the administration's important decisions with a view to how they would affect the construction of a lasting Republican majority. Nixon's White House was eager to wrap his proposals into grand concepts — the New Federalism, the Nixon Doctrine — and declare championships: the first this, the longest that, even if there was no grand concept behind the phrases.[43]

If there was a governing philosophy underlying Nixon's presidency, it was best explained in a paper written in 1970 by Nixon's speechwriter William Safire, with the tacit endorsement of Nixon, under the name of "Publius," in which Safire described Nixon's governing philosophy. Explaining Nixon's New Federalism, an attempt to decentralize government, Safire wrote, "In a proudly diverse, pluralistic society, what is 'in good conscience' in one place may be in bad conscience somewhere else. 'Good' men differ on marijuana, segregation, and the conflict of rights between free press and fair trial; what determines a 'national' conscience?" And then Safire came to the line that was blatantly reflective of the attitude of the Nixon presidency: "To the New Federalists, morality in a nation . . . is what most people who think about morality at all think is moral at a given time."[44]

Nixon not only liked to talk about leaders he had known — and later in life he wrote a book about them (*Leaders*) — but also was affected by their style.[45] He was a believer in the "Great Man" theory of history — the view, especially popular in the nineteenth century, that large events are created by extraordinary figures (such as Napoleon, Churchill, Hitler, or de Gaulle) rather than by economic or societal factors or an accumulation of events that lead to other events. He most admired French president Charles de Gaulle, who had led the resistance to the Nazis during World War II. De Gaulle was the one foreign leader to receive him in what Nixon called his "wilderness years" after 1962, when no one expected him to return to power. The tall, imposing de Gaulle had the grandeur that Nixon could only strive for. De Gaulle impressed Nixon as a man of vision, for his capacity for blending high intellect and instinct, his ability to create his own mystique, and also his strong preference for privacy. De Gaulle had written, Nixon pointed out admiringly and tellingly, that the three prerequisites of a leader were "mystery, character, and grandeur."[46] David Gergen, a Nixon speechwriter (who went on to serve three more presidents), wrote that Nixon's admiration for de Gaulle had its positive and negative effects. Trying to emulate de Gaulle expanded Nixon's vision and encouraged his search for grand strategies, but it also reinforced his fondness for pomp, and, according to Gergen, "reinforced his own worst instincts": his tendency toward isolation and aloofness and his failure to "observe the traditions of normal democratic politics." Nixon believed, Gergen wrote, that "the exercise of power is the same thing as the exercise of leadership."[47]

Unfortunately for him, Nixon faced a Democratic Congress throughout his presidency, which limited his exercise of power and frustrated him. When Nixon first took office, the Democrats controlled the Senate 57–43 and the House 242–190. In fact, Nixon was the first newly elected president since 1848 to face a Congress dominated by the opposition party. From the outset, Nixon and his team pitted themselves against the Democratic Congress and the press, though at first they actually felt intimidated by them.[48] Nixon was further hampered in his dealings with the Congress by his having no stomach for face-to-face confrontations. The Republican Party itself was divided between liberals (such as Charles "Mac" Mathias of Maryland, Edward Brooke of Massachusetts, John Sherman Cooper of Kentucky, and others) and those to the right of center, dependable Nixon supporters. Nixon loathed the liberal Republicans, many of whom came from distinguished families — calling them "phony liberals" — and most of his staff regarded Congress as a whole with contempt.[49] The Nixon people didn't mind alienating the liberal Republicans, or even driving them out of their party. It was all part of their attempt to reduce the influence of the "eastern elite" as they cultivated blue-collar workers. Though he often described himself as a "pragmatist," Nixon wrote in his book *In the Arena,* published in 1990,

"The worst kind of pragmatism is that practiced by the mushy moderate, who believes in nothing but what works and inevitably becomes a captive of Washington's permanent liberal establishment."[50]

Sometimes Nixon used others to carry out his dirty work against those he opposed. In the fall of 1970, in a series of speeches approved by Nixon, Vice President Agnew excoriated the press. Agnew's most famous speech, delivered in Des Moines, attacked the television networks and their "provincialism" as a result of being centered in New York and Washington, calling them an "unelected elite" and denouncing their practice of "instant rebuttal" following presidential speeches. (Nixon and the Reverend Billy Graham were later caught on tape agreeing that Jews had a "stranglehold" on the media.) Agnew's speeches, largely written at first by Safire, were characterized by alliterative phrases like "nattering nabobs of negativism." Other aides who joined in attacking the press were speechwriter Patrick Buchanan and political aide Charles Colson, both of whom became hatchet men for Nixon, bent on destroying the president's "enemies." The idea for the Des Moines speech was Buchanan's, and it echoed words Nixon had been using privately.[51]

Buchanan intimated that the administration might engage in "ideological antitrust" actions against newspaper companies that owned television stations — such as the Washington Post Company. In fact, there was an abortive effort to strip the Washington Post Company of its broadcasting licenses.[52] Nixon, furious over a report by CBS's Daniel Schorr, ordered the Internal Revenue Service to investigate him; when word of this spread, the administration claimed that this was just a routine background check because it was considering Schorr for a job.[53] Lead speechwriter Ray Price wrote later, "We did often lie, mislead, deceive, try to use [the press], and to con them."[54]

Though Nixon hated press conferences, considering them a waste of time, he sought to make a good impression on the public and prepared for them at length, memorizing the answers to expected questions in order to be able to talk without notes; he often came across as knowledgeable and thoughtful — Nixon was, after all, a very smart man — and he could turn in an impressive performance. But it didn't come as easily to him as it appeared: Evans and Novak wrote, "No president ever prepared so diligently for a press conference as Richard Nixon. . . . He would sit in a cool, dark room collecting his thoughts and calming himself, but when he entered the East Room of the White House for the press conference, he would often be bathed in sweat."

Nixon was almost constantly at work on his image. Though he could be rambling in conversations, he prepared as thoroughly for meetings as he did for speeches and press conferences, relying on his remarkable memory. He later proudly wrote that during his entire presidency, he never used a Tele-PrompTer.[55] Nixon could be an effective speaker, delivering his texts with authority and a strong speaking style. He also knew what to use a speech for. Over time, Nixon developed almost perfect pitch with respect to the hypocrisies that conventional people lived by — the fears they didn't admit, the hatred they wanted to express but couldn't, the images they would like to have of themselves — and had a sense of how to exploit all that.

Nixon told his press aides that it was important to stay on the offensive against the press.[56] His memos brimmed with strategies for handling both friendly and hostile journalists, and for polishing his own image.[57] Five days into his presidency, he instructed Ehrlichman to get out the word to the press that "RN has wit, is kind to his staff, that he works long hours, that people in his Cabinet and Security Council and all who come to see him are immensely impressed by his ability to preside over a meeting, to grasp a subject, that he reads an immense amount of material, etc." He also noted his image problems: "I've got to put on my nice-guy hat and dance at the White House . . . but let me be clear that it is not my nature."[58] But the physically clumsy Nixon lacked a capacity for the instinctive gesture; try as he did, he had a hard time looking relaxed. Once, in an attempt to emulate Robert Kennedy, he had himself photographed walking on the beach — in black wingtip shoes.

The thuggish side of the Nixon White House was on display in the first few months of the administration, as the Nixon command cynically strove to ensure the support of blue-collar workers by attacking antiwar protesters and showering praise on construction workers after they beat up antiwar demonstrators on Wall Street on May 8, 1969.[59] Nixon and Agnew praised the "Hard Hats," and Nixon later met with their leader in the White House and accepted a construction worker's hat; his longtime political strategist Murray Chotiner kept it on a table in his office tucked away in the East Wing. (Nixon later appointed the head of the construction workers' union, Peter Brennan, as his secretary of labor.) Keeping up the war in Vietnam and attacking antiwar demonstrators were conjoined with the administration's strategy for holding on to the support of blue-collar workers whom they weren't able to attract on economic issues.

Nixon unloosed Agnew to verbally attack antiwar demonstrators. In 1970, the vice president traveled to thirty states denouncing "Radiclibs," a term devised by Agnew himself and speechwriter Patrick Buchanan, denoting those who wanted the United States to get out of Vietnam, sought to reduce Pentagon spending, and were "weak" on law and order.[60] In early May 1971, during a large antiwar demonstration in Washington that was intended to shut down the government, ten thousand demonstrators were arrested and detained, in violation of their constitutional rights. The Mitchell Justice Department had advised that such action would be constitutional.[61]

To an unprecedented degree, Nixon was involved in the selection of Republican candidates for the midterm elections in 1970, as he and Chotiner devised a strategy of trying to elect more conservative Republicans to the Senate.[62] The effort was funded in large part by a secret multimillion-dollar slush fund, in what the Nixon people referred to as the "Town House Project," run by a former White House aide who worked out of the basement of a town house in Northwest Washington. But both Nixon's and Agnew's harsh campaign rhetoric in the fall of 1970 worked to their disadvantage. Agnew's strident and clumsy campaigning led to a spilling over of concerns about him that had been accumulating among Republican regulars, and the vice president was no longer welcome in several states. Nixon was said to have been disappointed in Agnew's campaigning and considered replacing him in 1972.[63]

In the final three weeks before the 1970 midterm election, Nixon himself stumped for Republican candidates in twenty-three states. This was what he loved to do, though he agonized about which states he could campaign in without attracting too much controversy.[64] On October 29, in San Jose, when Nixon was beset by antiwar demonstrators, he leaped on the hood of his car and lifted his arms in the V sign, hoping to turn this situation to his advantage. Some in the crowd responded by throwing rocks, flags, and candles, a few of which struck the president.[65] His election-eve speech consisted of a tape of a speech he'd given in Phoenix on October 31, in which he excoriated the "violent thugs" who had attacked him and was particularly raspy about law and order — the scene had been caught on a grainy film with poor sound, which made it look all the grimmer. Nixon's performance stood in sharp contrast to that of Edmund Muskie, Humphrey's 1968 running mate (and presumed presidential candidate for the 1972 election); Muskie, looking Lincolnesque in a large wingback chair, called on the voters to reject the "politics of fear." The contrast damaged the Republicans, and Nixon, badly. It was Muskie, not Nixon, who appeared presidential.

The results of the 1970 elections were a disappointment for the Republicans, who picked up only two of the seven Senate seats they needed to gain the majority — though for the incumbent party in the White House to gain seats in an off-year election was a reversal of a historical trend. The Republicans also lost a net of eleven governorships and nine House seats.[66] Although Nixon and his aides purveyed the notion that the election results were a triumph, the Nixon presidency was at a low point.[67] The result was a reassessment by Nixon and his aides and a decision that the president should abandon his hermitlike ways and stress more positive ideas, concentrating more on domestic programs. But this, like other efforts to portray Nixon as a positive, forward-looking president, was less than totally successful.

At the same time Nixon had become dissatisfied with his cabinet overall. Even early in his presidency he came to realize that most of his cabinet secretaries were discontented most of the time, and he felt that they were poor managers who had become captives of their bureaucracies. Ehrlichman wrote that Nixon called the complainers "crybabies." (Cabinet meetings bored him anyway.) So Nixon and his aides embarked on several efforts to make the cabinet more responsive to the White House. A presidential aide said, "It works in the Vatican. It works in the mafia. It ought to work here."[68] Gradually, Nixon turned over the duties of some cabinet secretaries to members of the White House staff.[69]

And so, after the 1970 election, the Nixon

White House drew up a purge list, starting with Interior Secretary Walter Hickel, a former governor of Alaska, who had infuriated Nixon and his aides by his outspokenness on issues outside his department's purview — especially in his sympathy with campus antiwar activists and opposition to the invasion of Cambodia — and by his transformation from the antienvironmentalism he had expressed when he was appointed to a growing sympathy toward the environmental movement. Worse, in May 1970 Hickel had sent Nixon an impassioned letter accusing the administration of lacking "appropriate concern" for young people, and the letter leaked to the press. Nixon and his closest aides decided forthwith that Hickel had to be sacked. But by then Hickel had a national constituency, so the deed was put off until after the 1970 election.[70] Though he talked incessantly about getting rid of people, Nixon actually had a hard time doing so, and whenever possible left the job to others. And this was at a time when Nixon was trying once again to cultivate a positive image. But the Nixon administration had difficulty firing people cleanly. When, after the election, Mitchell told Hickel he should leave, Hickel simply refused, so that a highly uncomfortable

Nixon was forced to do it. Normally, cabinet officers were not fired; they were asked to "resign," so the White House announcement that Hickel had been forced out stirred a storm of protest.

Nixon had also targeted HUD Secretary George Romney, an intense, bombastic man and former auto executive who pressed hard for more money for the cities, more low-cost housing, and — most distressful to the White House — racial integration of white suburbs. Romney resisted John Mitchell's suggestion that he leave, saying that only the president could tell him to do so, but Nixon had no stomach for facing him down, particularly after the fuss caused by Hickel's firing, so Romney stayed. Romney himself was puzzled by the Nixon White House and "the Germans," as Haldeman and Ehrlichman were widely referred to.[71] Also in 1970, on Nixon's orders, Fred Malek, the head of Nixon's personnel office, targeted sixty-two appointees for removal. Even after Malek's purges, which continued in 1971, Nixon complained, "We've checked and found that 96 percent of the bureaucracy are against us; they're bastards who are here to screw us."[72] At another point, Nixon instructed Malek to count the number of Jews who were employed by the Bureau of Labor Statistics, which he believed was rigging unemployment figures to make him look bad. Malek carried out the order.[73]

Nixon's advisers were divided between those who argued that he should be a reconciler — the theme of his victory speech in 1968 was "Bring Us Together" — and those, in particular John Mitchell, who argued that the key to reelection was holding on to his 1968 voters and adding those who had supported Wallace. Evans and Novak reported that Nixon believed in both approaches.[74] The White House strategy was strongly influenced by two influential books: Kevin Phillips's *The Emerging Republican Majority* and Richard M. Scammon and Ben J. Wattenberg's *The Real Majority;* Scammon and Wattenberg argued that the American political majority was "unyoung, unblack, and unpoor,"[75] a conclusion that encouraged Nixon to continue to emphasize "law and order" as a campaign theme and pay little attention to minorities.

Earlier in his career, Nixon had portrayed himself as fairly progressive on civil rights — he was supposedly affected by his exposure to minorities while at a southern law school and in the navy — but now it was different. Pragmatism called; politics ruled. And over time, the country was to learn of his private views, which showed him to be a bigoted man. He spoke privately of blacks as "just down out of the trees" and expressed other racist views; he put no blacks in his cabinet or White House and ordered that the White House waiters should not continue to be all blacks.[76] To hold together his coalition of southerners and blue-collar workers, Nixon spoke out against "forced busing" and talked often about "crime in the streets" — code for black agitation as well as another take on "law and order."

After a discussion with Nixon at Camp David about civil rights, Haldeman wrote in his diary on August 9, 1970, "The P [President] has changed his mind, reached a new conclusion. Is convinced policy of sucking after left won't work, not only can't win them, can't even diffuse them. Wants E [Ehrlichman] to shape policies so as to move our way. P changed his mind about school desegregation statement of March 24, thinks it went too far."[77] Nixon made no effort to push the Justice Department to enforce the civil rights laws. (Mitchell, of course, was in on this strategy.) While there was some progress on civil rights in the course of the Nixon presidency, it was not at the behest of the administration itself, and the subject was treated with more than a little cynicism. The Justice Department, by contrast, did enforce court rulings on civil rights, and by the time Nixon left office there was little segregation in southern public schools, but Nixon and his aides were careful not to brag about this, letting the Democrats and the courts take the "blame." Nixon told an aide, "I think if we can keep liberal writers convinced that we are doing what the Court requires, and our conservative friends convinced that we are not doing any more than the Court requires, I think we can walk this tightrope until November, 1972."[78] But on the specific issue of busing, Nixon wasn't prepared to give in to the courts over the protests of his southern and blue-collar constituency, so he spoke out angrily against "forced busing" and pushed for a constitutional amendment against it. (Though such an amendment was never adopted, in July 1974 a more conservative-leaning court, due to Nixon's appointments, essentially invalidated an earlier court decision that allowed busing.)[79] He fired Leon Panetta (later to be a Democratic congressman and Bill Clinton's chief of staff) from his job as head of HEW's civil rights division, for his outspoken complaints that the administration was moving too slowly on civil rights. The White House also slowed down efforts by George Romney's Department of Housing and Urban Development to push for desegregation of all-white suburbs.

There was one anomaly in the administration's general effort to drag its heels on desegregation. At the urging of Labor Secretary George Shultz, Nixon did revive, in a milder form, a Democratic program, known as the "Philadelphia Plan," which set goals and timetables for employing minority workers on federally funded projects, and ordered the construction unions to train young blacks as apprentices. The union leaders minded this less than they had the Democratic plan, and Nixon received less credit for it than his people thought he deserved, principally because his rhetoric and tone and other actions on race issues made it clear that he was on the side of antiblack southerners and blue-collar workers — of the white majority and the status quo. His real constituency understood that, and he remained deeply unpopular with black voters. Despite the progress that was made on integration, essentially by the courts, while he was president Nixon ended up furthering racial division in the country.[80]

To further please the South, Nixon nominated for the Supreme Court Clement F. Haynsworth Jr., a federal appeals court judge from Greenville, South Carolina (Strom Thurmond's home state), who was conservative on civil rights. Enough members of both parties were opposed to the Haynsworth nomination that the Senate — despite Nixon's strenuous efforts — voted it down on November 21, 1969, making Haynsworth the first Supreme Court nominee since 1930 to be rejected by the Senate. Despite the defeat, Nixon actually saw a possible political benefit from having fought for Haynsworth and blaming the "liberals" for voting him down. Next, in January 1970 he deliberately picked as his Supreme Court nominee a man even more anti–civil rights, the highly undistinguished federal appeals court judge G. Harrold Carswell from Florida, who in 1948 had openly endorsed segregation. Several Republican senators urged Nixon to withdraw this embarrassment of a nomination, but Nixon, whose back was up, refused, and the White House's crude tactics to get Carswell approved only made things worse. Carswell's nomination also went down to defeat in the Senate in

April 1970. (It was Carswell's nomination that prompted Senator Roman Hruska of Nebraska to issue his famous dictum that even if Carswell was mediocre, mediocre people "are entitled to a little representation.") A furious Nixon removed from the White House guest list the names of some Republicans who had voted against Carswell. But he had shown the South that he was on its side.[81] In a major irony, Nixon's next nominee was Harry Blackmun, who, Nixon had been assured, was a safe choice. Though Nixon had campaigned against "abortion on demand" — another example of his propensity, and dark talent, for loaded terminology — Blackmun was, of course, to be the author of the landmark 1973 *Roe v. Wade* decision, holding that women had a constitutional right to abortions in the first trimester.[82]

Long and hard as he had worked for it, Nixon often escaped from the presidency and all its demands. By seven months into the job, he virtually abandoned Washington, his staff, the Congress, the press — spending as much time out of the capital as he could. He vacationed quite often with Bebe Rebozo, a newly wealthy Florida real estate speculator who owned the dominant bank in Key Biscayne, and Rebozo's friend Robert Abplanalp, the millionaire inventor of the aerosol valve, who had a home in the Bahamas. Nixon spent much of his vacation time with his two pals in Key Biscayne, Florida, where he, with Rebozo's help, bought two bungalows, next door to Rebozo's house. Nixon also purchased a retreat in San Clemente, California, a $340,000 home overlooking the Pacific.[83] Rebozo and Abplanalp helped Nixon finance his San Clemente property and paid for improvements on the California and Florida houses.[84] Abplanalp, Rebozo, and Nixon often went out on Abplanalp's boat, the *Coco Lobo.* Nixon also spent a great deal of time at Camp David — where he went without Mrs. Nixon but was often accompanied by the hard-drinking, pugnacious Rebozo. Nixon especially appreciated Rebozo's companionship because Rebozo could keep silent, as Nixon wished. The two men could spend hours together without speaking, until Nixon chose to talk. They drank together, watched movies together, and sometimes engaged in sophomoric tricks.

Essentially, Nixon remained the loner he had been since childhood. Even his dog didn't like him. The staff once laid a trail of biscuits to lure his Irish setter King Tima-hoe to Nixon's desk in order to entice him to get closer to his owner.[85] But the dog wouldn't move.

In their book *Nixon in the White House,* Evans and Novak provided perhaps the most pointed assessment of the man at the center of the American political system: "Never having made his reputation as a politician emotionally wedded to controversial and powerful causes . . . Nixon came to office curiously unfathomed as a human being even to party leaders who composed his base of support. For Nixon the politician, far more than Lyndon Johnson or John F. Kennedy or Dwight Eisenhower, concealed Nixon the man, and the man was, even to some of his close friends, an unbelievably complex, shy, remote and tense figure."[86]

4
THE PRAGMATIST

Numerous people have attempted to dress
up Richard Nixon's domestic policy in a
unifying philosophy: He was a "progressive"; he was "the last liberal." But the
"liberal" or "progressive" attributions are
largely a matter of hindsight — formed in
the context of more conservative presidencies and different, post-Reagan times, and
the conservative if not radical presidency of
George W. Bush. In reality, Nixon's domestic policy was a blend of the enlightened
and the opportunistic. There was in fact no
guiding philosophy. In 1969, a Republican
senator referred to Nixon as "the man with
the portable center."[1] John Ehrlichman
described Nixon as an a priori conservative,
and, according to his own account, by 1970
Ehrlichman himself was struggling against
the more conservative of Nixon's advisers
— and Nixon himself — to keep the president from swerving even more to the right.[2]

At the start of Nixon's second term, John Mitchell said, perhaps in part to please the core constituency, "This country is going so far to the right you won't recognize it."[3]

Nixon described himself as a "pragmatist," and he should be taken at his word.[4] George Romney told a friend, "I don't know what the president believes in. Maybe he doesn't believe in anything." Nixon's biographer Melvin Small observed that "it is quite likely that a Democratic administration, backed by a Democratic Congress, would have adopted many of the Nixon administration's approaches" to the economy, the Great Society, and the environment. "But it is difficult to imagine a Democratic administration dealing with those problems in such a cynical and completely political fashion."[5] In his book *Nixon's Shadow,* David Greenberg wrote of the fashion of retrospectively viewing Nixon as a liberal: "In 1972, someone describing Nixon as liberal in domestic policy would have been laughed at." He also points out, "The President routinely described himself as a conservative, in favor of a smaller government, traditional values, and private business, and pitted himself in direct contrast to the liberals."[6]

Nixon's domestic policy has to be seen in

the context of his times. In the forties and the fifties, World War II and the Cold War had buried domestic conflict. (McCarthyism was the exception.) Those decades were the age of conformity, of men in gray flannel suits — the period of "the end of ideology," in the words of the sociologist Daniel Bell. The sixties began quietly; the urban unrest and antiwar protests were to come later. Left and Right largely accepted the New Deal and were anticommunist.[7] John F. Kennedy was largely content to preserve this consensus. When Lyndon Johnson took the place of the fallen president, he pushed hard for some domestic policies that Kennedy had begun to champion before his assassination, particularly on civil rights, which Johnson went on to expand. In a speech in Ann Arbor, Michigan, in May 1964, he set forth his Great Society, a sweeping vision of using government to try to improve Americans' lives. With his landslide victory over Barry Goldwater that fall, Johnson was able to enact much of his program into law, including an ambitious "War on Poverty." But by 1968, not only was Johnson facing strong opposition to the Vietnam War, but also, as he understood, he had overreached in seeking so many new domestic programs, and his Great Society was losing steam — and acceptance. The antiwar protests of the late 1960s and the racial violence that had broken out in several cities, plus the growing costs of the Vietnam War, were also making domestic programs less attractive to the American people.

Starting before Nixon came to office, there was also a growing concern in Congress, even among many Democrats, including several former Johnson administration officials, that there were too many "categorical" programs — too many individual programs to deal with this or that specific social problem. A kind of fatigue had set in on Capitol Hill.[8] In time, there was also a spreading view that the programs weren't working. It was too soon to make such an overall judgment, but in fact some of them were not working as well as their proponents had hoped. A number of programs, in the view of Johnson budget director Charles Schultze, had been born of idealism and isolated anecdotal success stories — what he called at the time the *"Reader's Digest syndrome"* — and easy optimism. And there was at the time a kind of fatigue of liberalism. Nixon in fact came to office at a transitional time and was a transitional figure. On both foreign policy (the Cold

War) and domestic policy, it was time for a rethink — which Nixon understood, accepted, and implemented.[9]

Given the fact that Nixon faced a Democratic Congress, he "had to be pragmatic if he wanted to get anything done," as Small observed.[10] At the time, the Nixon administration seemed to be less defined in terms of the philosophy of its governing than of its technique, which was ad hoc. To the new administration, improvisation bought time.[11] Because of his politics and his disdain for moderate politicians, not to mention liberal Democrats, Nixon "avoided the liberal-moderate coalition that was there for the asking," wrote the journalist John Osborne.[12] His environmental policies, for which he was much praised in hindsight, had a strong vein of pragmatism, even opportunism. Garry Wills wrote in *Nixon Agonistes* that Nixon not only had an affinity for Woodrow Wilson but he thought of himself as a Wilsonian in both his domestic and foreign policies: at home, both believed in the self-made man — a laissez-faire philosophy, Wills pointed out, that preceded the New Deal — and in internationalism abroad.[13] Wills also wrote that Nixon likened himself to Wilson as an introspective intellectual, the "lonely misunderstood leader."[14] (Nixon even appropriated Wilson's desk from the vice president's office on Capitol Hill for his own use in the Oval Office. He later discovered that the desk had actually belonged to Henry Wilson, Ulysses S. Grant's vice president.)[15]

Nixon believed in the individual — in Wills's terms, in the "mystique of the worker,"[16] the striving common man, the Horatio Alger myth. Evans and Novak noted that Nixon had an idealistic streak, but that his interest in domestic policy was "intermittent and secondary."[17] According to Nixon domestic policy aide Christopher DeMuth, Nixon "wanted to manage things sufficiently so that he could buy time and discretion to deal with foreign affairs, where he did have a sense of where he wanted to go."[18]

Nixon's indecisiveness was one factor in his initially hesitant approach to domestic policy. As Osborne observed in the *New Republic* in March 1969, the Nixon White House was "feeling the heat" to produce some sort of domestic action, some initiative. "They also sensed," wrote Osborne, "and loyally tried to conceal, a certain indecision in the president himself; a tendency, continuing in the third month of his Administration, to grasp at one excuse after another to postpone his choices" among options that had been presented to him.[19] Nixon blamed his staff for the delay.

Even when Nixon felt compelled in 1970, for political reasons, to show more interest in domestic issues, Evans and Novak wrote, "Despite his heralded change toward a new concentration on domestic affairs, his political aides complained that he did not stir himself on key congressional votes in Congress as he did on foreign policy questions."[20] Small quotes Nixon telling his staff, "I am only interested when we make a major breakthrough or have a major failure. Otherwise don't bother me."[21] Though he made some proposals in 1969, Nixon decided to focus on domestic issues only after the Republicans didn't do as well as he'd hoped in the 1970 midterm elections. The only domestic issues that Nixon was truly interested in, Ehrlichman wrote, were those he believed were "potent political medicine." Therefore, according to Ehrlichman, Nixon took personal charge of all such politically loaded issues as abortion, race, aid to parochial schools, labor legislation, drugs, crime, welfare, and taxes. Other issues, in particular the environment, health care, campus unrest, transportation, and housing, he delegated to others.[22] Gerald

Ford told Small that Nixon was "so much more enamored with foreign policy" that he left congressional affairs to an "evil group" composed of Haldeman, Ehrlichman, and Colson.[23]

When Nixon came to office in 1969, the environmental movement was reaching its peak and had strong advocates in Congress — especially Democratic senators Edmund Muskie of Maine and Gaylord Nelson of Wisconsin, an environmental crusader for his entire political life and even after he left office. Events also propelled the movement. Rachel Carson had published her phenomenal bestseller *Silent Spring* in 1962; Paul Ehrlich published his book *The Population Bomb* in 1969; in January 1969, an oil spill spoiled the California coastline for some time, and later that year the Cuyahoga River, in Cleveland, caught fire. The American public was becoming increasingly concerned about pollution of the air and water, and Nelson had been pressing for legislation to deal with the problems.

As a stopgap measure in 1969, Nixon, preoccupied by other matters, set up a token environmental agency, but Congress was far from satisfied. On New Year's Day 1970, with a great flourish, proclaiming himself an environmentalist, Nixon signed a sweeping act passed by Congress, the National Environmental Protection Act, which established a national environmental policy and called for a new office in the Executive Office of the President to review, propose, and consolidate environmental programs.

In the weeks leading up to his 1970 State of the Union address, Nixon called for several polls and found that the public's concern about the environment had risen from 25 percent in 1965 to 75 percent toward the end of 1969.[24] So, in his speech to Congress Nixon proposed thirty-eight environmental measures, several of which had already been put forward by the environmentalists on Capitol Hill, though their proposals were often more comprehensive than Nixon's.

In April 1970 the nation celebrated Earth Day, Gaylord Nelson's idea, in which millions of Americans participated. Though even White House aides joined in cleaning up the Potomac River, Nixon offered no proclamation. He turned the environmental issue over to Ehrlichman, telling him, "Just keep me out of trouble on environmental issues," and privately he continued to make derogatory, often profane, comments about the movement, calling it "overrated" and "crap" for "clowns."[25] Ehrlichman wrote, "He preferred to stay away from the environmental issues . . . free to criticize, taking bows when things went well."[26] The following summer, as part of a larger effort to reorganize federal agencies, Nixon proposed legislation creating the Environmental Protection Agency, and he named forceful environmentalists — William Ruckelshaus and after him Russell Train — to run it.

According to Nixon's chief White House environmental adviser, John Whitaker, the Nixon White House sought to strike a "balance" between what the Democratic Congress was proposing and what Nixon's business constituency preferred, and Nixon only reluctantly signed the more progressive environmental bills that Congress sent to his desk.

Still, under Nixon and the Democratic Congress, a number of new environmental laws were enacted: a bill to strengthen the Clean Air Act of 1967, setting higher standards for auto emissions, though not by as much as Muskie and others had proposed. Muskie, the original sponsor of the Clean Air Act, wasn't even invited to the White House signing ceremony. (Nixon later eased the standards during the energy crisis of 1974.) In 1972, Nixon also signed into law the Clean Water Act, to help salvage polluted rivers, having vetoed the first version of this bill passed by Congress as too expensive and, after being overridden he withheld — "impounded" — most of the funds Congress authorized for it. He also signed the Coastal Zone Management Act, to protect estuaries; measures to increase U.S. participation in international environmental programs and to expand the number of public parks, placing many of them near cities (to appeal to the middle class); the Safe Drinking Water Act; and the Endangered Species Act. But Nixon did oppose some measures. His administration lost a court fight and was forced to ban the use of the pesticide DDT in the United States (but its sale overseas was still permitted). And, in what opponents saw as a cave-in to the soap and detergent industry, the administration successfully resisted regulation of phosphates in water, despite recommendations for regulation from his own environmental council.[27] As for Nixon's overall environmental record, the former Conservative member of the British Parliament Jonathan Aitken wrote in his admiring book about Nixon, "Although a late and at times reluctant convert to the causes of the conservation movement, he nevertheless delivered more results to it than any other president before or since."[28] In all, whatever his motives and his positioning, Nixon presided over a historical expansion of environmental protection in the United States. Gaylord Nelson himself expressed gratitude for Nixon's identifying himself with the issue, and the 1970s became known as "the environmental decade," even though there was considerable backsliding during the Ford administration, when Gerald Ford's chief of staff, Dick Cheney, was in charge of environmental policy.[29]

One of the most significant domestic efforts by the Nixon administration was to reform the nation's welfare laws. In 1969, the resourceful and creative Daniel Patrick Moynihan, the former Harvard professor now serving as the White House urban affairs adviser, convinced Nixon that he could be a latter-day Benjamin Disraeli, the reforming Conservative prime minister during the reign of Queen Victoria. Moynihan told Nixon that Disraeli proposed policies that Liberals would never dare to offer or hope to pass, and thus won middle-class support for his Tory Party. This strategy distressed other Nixon aides, including John Ehrlichman, who considered Moynihan a "left-winger." Yet, as a result of Moynihan's coaxing, in a nationwide television appearance on August 8, 1969, Nixon proposed the sweeping Family Assistance Plan, to replace welfare programs with cash payments. Moynihan had sold the idea to Nixon as a conservative one, and Nixon was also attracted to the idea that it would "get rid of social workers" and reduce the size and power of the federal bureaucracy.[30] Not only did Nixon hate the bureaucracy, but he was also shrewdly playing upon an incipient national desire to get the social planners, with their big ideas and rules and taxes, off the people's backs. In his 1968 presidential campaign, Nixon had expressed horror at the prospect of expanding the welfare rolls, a matter of concern to the middle-class workers he was cultivating, and his opposition to an income-maintenance program such as the Democrats were proposing. He had explicitly campaigned against cash payments to the poor.[31] California governor Ronald Reagan had successfully used the issue ("welfare queens") in his 1966 gubernatorial campaign and made real inroads on the votes of the white working class, and Nixon and his strategists saw an antiwelfare position as a way of building a Republican majority.

At the time, both liberals and conservatives disliked the existing welfare program, but for different reasons — which provided Nixon an opening but also spelled trouble for any proposal to revise it. Nixon's proposal changed the entire frame of reference in which welfare was discussed. It offered cash payments to the poor, national criteria for determining eligibility, and replacing intrusive welfare workers with the impartial and more automatic Social Security Administration. Nixon also tempered the liberal nature of his proposal by including work requirements for welfare recipients. Nevertheless, conservatives opposed it and liberals were disturbed by its flaws and the fact that the proposed income maintenance was only $1,600 a year. But though Nixon drew great attention to his grand proposal by announcing it on television, he was utterly cynical about it; Haldeman's diary entry on July 13, 1970, reads: "About Family Assistance Plan, [Nixon] wants to be sure it's killed by Democrats and that we make a big play for it, but don't let it pass, can't afford it."[32] Nixon's proposal to overhaul welfare policy died in Congress in 1970, and though he offered it again in later State of the Union speeches, he put no effort behind it and considered it dead.

The Great Society's poverty program was whittled down, but not by as much as Nixon wished. The head of the Office of Economic Opportunity, Donald Rumsfeld, worked to save the program, though he participated in eliminating some parts of it. Under Nixon the élan of the "war on poverty" faded. Nixon also opposed federal housing programs, and in 1973 he stopped requesting funds for them. On the other hand, he increased funding for education and, in his second term, proposed federal support for health insurance programs, especially for low-income families. (Nixon often referred to his parents' struggles to pay for health care.) But like the Family Assistance Plan, Nixon's health proposal failed in the face of opposition by conservatives (and the American Medical Association) who thought it went too far and liberals who didn't think it went far enough. He signed into law the Coal Mine Safety and Health Act, and a bill to establish the Occupational Safety and Health Administration, though the labor unions complained that it tilted too much toward business.

In the 1960s Democratic senators Robert Kennedy, Walter Mondale, and George McGovern had thrown the spotlight on the fact that poor people were going hungry in

America, and the issue loomed as one that could affect the 1970 midterm elections. So in the spring of 1969, Nixon called for an end to hunger in America and sponsored a White House conference on hunger, but he and his aides were angered by the result: Conferees attacked his food proposals as inadequate and called for more extensive federal food aid than Nixon was prepared to seek. He did expand the food stamp and school lunch programs, though he tempered his rhetoric on the subject so as not to upset conservatives, and later he sought to pare funds for feeding the hungry. The program, in fact, was deeply flawed. Evans and Novak wrote, "The hunger issue had shown the limitations of the Tory playing radical reformer, Nixon-style."[33] Nevertheless, by the end of his presidency, the number of Americans living below the poverty level had dropped, and aid to the poor had increased considerably.[34]

In the end, Nixon, who had run against the Great Society in 1968, and argued, as Republicans had since the 1930s, that government should be smaller, presided over a large expansion of domestic programs. The Democratic Congress stopped him from cutting some programs to the extent that he wished. At the beginning of his second term, not having to face the voters again, Nixon sought deeper cuts in domestic programs, but he didn't get very far because he was distracted by the events that led to the end of his presidency. Yet in the course of the Nixon presidency, spending on domestic programs had risen by more than $80 billion, in part because of the expansion of certain programs, in part as a result of built-in growth of other programs, and of inflation, and the gradual withdrawal of American troops from Vietnam. (Though the "peace dividend" didn't come close to what had been expected.)

Seeking new power to cut funds, in 1973 Nixon claimed an inherent right of the president to impound money appropriated by Congress, refusing to spend nearly 20 percent of the money authorized for more than one hundred programs, sometimes withholding the funds for an entire program that he did not like. Previous presidents had impounded funds — but to nowhere near the extent that Nixon did. Finally, in 1974, as Nixon was losing strength, Congress passed a law making it far more difficult for a president to impound funds, and in 1975 the Supreme Court ruled that a president didn't have the inherent right to impound.[35]

In a further effort to weaken federal programs and limit the power of the bureaucracy, Nixon also proposed a plan for "special revenue sharing," which would combine groups of categorical programs into "block grants" to state and local governments. Even before Nixon took office, some leading Democratic figures had already proposed combining separate federal programs into large categories, such as health or housing. Nixon picked up this proposal. What proponents were up against were the bureaucracies that administered the programs, the interest groups that benefited from them, and the congressional committees that had jurisdiction over them. Under Nixon's proposal, federal funding for most of the programs themselves was not to be cut (such large slashes weren't attempted until the Reagan administration), but still Nixon's proposal — which the administration described as returning "power to the people" — was intended to appease those involved in the "tax revolt" that was stirring at the state level as well as loosen the federal strings on such programs and reduce the strength of their constituencies. Since Nixon liked grand concepts, this idea was offered in 1971 in the name the New Federalism, which later became the

New American Revolution. The idea was to reduce paperwork and the size of the federal bureaucracy and get the decision making "closer to the people." But many liberals, suspicious that the states wouldn't observe the standards and rules set by the federal government, and concerned that they would spend the money on programs other than for the poor, opposed the block-grant program vigorously. After a protracted fight with Congress, during which Nixon became fainthearted for a time — but was spurred on by Ehrlichman — the administration won a partial victory. As it turned out, the mayors liked some of the programs, such as aid to the cities, and they survived, while other programs languished under block grants.

Nixon showed more interest in one domestic area, the economy, than he did in others. He inherited strong inflation from the Johnson presidency, and in a few months was also facing a recession and rising unemployment and the first trade deficit in the twentieth century.[36] This "stagflation" threatened to ruin his presidency. At first, Nixon eagerly and publicly abandoned the use of presidential pressure to hold down wages and prices, such as Johnson had exercised successfully for a time.[37] Nixon first tried what became known as "gradualism" to deal with the problem. But after an effort to "jawbone" business and labor to hold down wages and prices failed, and declaring "guideposts" didn't work, either, Nixon, who was otherwise seeking a reduction of the role of the federal government, in 1970 reluctantly accepted the idea of a ninety-day freeze on wages and prices. But he had no plan for what to do after the ninety days. Nixon later wrote that he temporarily imposed the wage and price controls for political reasons.[38] The controls were gradually relaxed, with the result that Nixon's presidency ended with higher inflation than when he entered the White House (8.7 percent versus just under 5 percent) as well as higher unemployment (5.6 percent versus 3.5 percent).[39] In essence, his economic policies didn't work. To help reverse the trade deficit, he removed America from the gold standard, thus devaluing the dollar. But Nixon's interest in international economics was limited. After the tapes of his conversations with aides were released during his impeachment ordeal, one line that became famous was, "I don't give a shit about the lira."

Several other expansions of federal activities and numerous innovations occurred under Nixon, whatever their origins or Nixon's motivations: establishing the first Office of Consumer Affairs in the White House and a new law, the Consumer Protection Act; the funding of Amtrak; the constitutional amendment granting eighteen-year-olds the right to vote; the end of the draft; and large increases in federal funds to support the arts.

Moreover, as a result of new laws enacted during his time in office, Nixon presided over a dramatic expansion of the regulatory state. The New Deal had established the idea of a larger role for the federal government, to be sure, but the thrust of the New Deal was to restore economic stability and jobs. The environmental, job-safety, highway-safety, consumer-protection laws that Nixon approved instructed private companies on how to conduct their business. This was a new departure. Nixon probably didn't intend to expand the role and power of the federal government in this way but, cumulatively, it happened with his approval.

And so, rail as he did against "big government," in particular the Great Society, in the end Nixon accepted its premise: that the federal government can do good things for the people. He was the last Republican president to do so.

5
THE FOREIGN POLICY PRESIDENT

Richard Nixon was also a pragmatist on foreign policy. While publicly he burnished his credentials as a hard-line anticommunist, he resisted calls from the Republican right to "roll back the iron curtain" and took bold and imaginative steps to improve U.S. relationships with Russia and China. Like his chief foreign policy adviser Henry Kissinger, Nixon believed in "realpolitik" in the model of the nineteenth-century Austrian statesman Metternich, whom Kissinger greatly admired (and was the subject of his Ph.D. dissertation at Harvard). Metternich's theory placed great emphasis on the state's interests and the use of military force to achieve them; it also included a preference for dealing with strong leaders of nations that could aid in the pursuit of these interests. In an argument that was to rend American policy makers for a long time, Nixon and Kissinger preferred stability over reform. They favored strong but flawed, corrupt, and ultimately unstable regimes headed by such figures as the Shah of Iran, Philippines strongman Ferdinand Marcos, and South Vietnam president Nguyen Van Thieu.

Nixon attained great achievements in foreign policy, but close examination presents a contradictory picture of a man who could give long, thoughtful disquisitions and produce lucid conceptualizations about world affairs, while at the same time his actual policy making was often marked by fits and starts, by rages and impulsiveness, and by major gaps in his attention — with his own inner turmoil having an effect on some of his policies. Nixon had traveled widely as vice president, and he came to office considering himself an expert on foreign policy and wanted to be defined as a foreign policy president. He eagerly sought the role of world statesman, and foreign travel provided a break from the less attractive business of governing. He ended up taking more foreign trips by far than any other president and holding an unprecedented number of state dinners.[1] But Nixon was serious about having an impact on international affairs and intent on rearranging great power relationships. He sought to break the grip of the Cold War on U.S. international policies. In important, historic ways, this approach was successful. But he also made a large, tragic mistake.

After the fact, the word "Vietnam" became a metaphor for a misguided military venture: a quagmire, a policy misconception, a failure — and also politically ruinous. In that sense, Vietnam was Richard Nixon's Vietnam. The venture had been begun and extended by his predecessors John F. Kennedy and Lyndon Johnson, and it had led to Johnson's not seeking reelection. Over time, Nixon was awarded much praise for withdrawing American troops from Vietnam, and all but ending the war (though it didn't officially end until 1975, after Nixon had left office). Kissinger received the Nobel Peace Prize in 1973 for negotiating a cease-fire agreement with North Vietnam. But there remained the lingering question of whether it was worth it to carry on the war for nearly five more years and to expand it to neighboring countries, in particular Cambodia, at the cost of many thousands more American lives as well as those of countless Southeast Asians. And as it went on, Nixon's Vietnam policies stirred ever-larger antiwar protests, divided the country, and contributed to the public's loss of trust in government. Though the Pentagon Papers were a mammoth study of decision making on Vietnam during the Johnson administration, they raised serious questions about overall U.S. policy in Vietnam, and Nixon was determined to punish the leaker.

When Nixon took office in 1969, the United States had more than 530,000 troops in Vietnam. Kennedy had sent 16,000 "advisers" (plus helicopters, planes, and other equipment), and in 1965 Johnson introduced ground troops. Their number kept rising, as did the deaths of American servicemen there — more than 30,000 by the time Nixon took office. Johnson's serial escalations of the U.S. involvement in Vietnam not only stirred up a strong antiwar movement, but also raised serious doubts about the war among foreign policy officials and on Capitol Hill. Johnson himself became ambivalent about the war and in early 1968, on the advice of his new secretary of defense Clark Clifford and other elder statesmen such as former secretary of state Dean Acheson, Johnson became convinced that the war had to be wound down; he halted the escalation and turned down his generals' request for another 206,000 troops. On March 31, 1968, he announced a reduction of air strikes on North Vietnam, authorized the opening of peace talks with the North Vietnamese — and announced that he wouldn't run for reelection.

After a lengthy stalemate in the talks, the North Vietnamese offered to expand them to include the Vietcong and the South Vietnamese if the bombing of North Vietnam was halted. On October 31, 1968, Johnson announced a total cessation of the bombing of North Vietnam in the hopes of pacifying the antiwar movement, making some progress in the Paris peace talks, and helping Hubert Humphrey (if not soon enough).

Through Kissinger, Nixon and his campaign manager John Mitchell got wind of the fact that Johnson was planning a bombing halt.[2] Ostensibly a Humphrey adviser, Kissinger was also giving the Nixon camp foreign policy advice and providing it with information about Humphrey's plans — though in private Kissinger spoke about Nixon scathingly. Nixon and Mitchell had already been in contact with Anna Chennault, the Chinese-born widow of the World War II ace pilot Claire Chennault and the chairwoman of the Women for Nixon Committee, who had close ties to the South Vietnamese government. Through Chennault, Nixon sent word to the South Vietnamese encouraging them to go slow in the peace talks and to assure them that they would receive more support from a President Nixon. Two days after Johnson's announcement, the South Vietnamese let it be known that they wouldn't meet in Paris with representatives of the Vietcong. (It has remained a matter of speculation as to whether they would have done the same thing without Mrs. Chennault's intervention.)

Asked by a reporter as he was campaigning in New Hampshire in March 1968 if he had a "secret plan" for ending the war in Vietnam, Nixon replied, "Yes," and said, "I have a plan to end the war." Though Nixon himself didn't actually use the term "secret plan," it stuck with him, to his annoyance. Nixon also said that he couldn't reveal the plan for fear of undercutting the president.

But there was no plan.

When Nixon chose Kissinger as his national security adviser, the two men shared the same goal: to concentrate the management of foreign policy in the White House. Not only did Nixon distrust the foreign policy bureaucracy — he remarked that he didn't want foreign policy run by the "striped-pants faggots in Foggy Bottom"[3] — he also didn't want a strong secretary of state, such as Eisenhower's powerful John Foster Dulles. Kissinger, for his part, wanted to accrue as much power for himself as he could. So, in contrast with Nixon's hesitant approach to domestic concerns, Nixon and Kissinger quickly set up their own national security apparatus in the White House. The size of the National Security Council staff was significantly increased, and the roles of other agencies involved in foreign policy — the State Department, the Defense Department, and the CIA — were greatly reduced. The new secretary of state, William Rogers, Nixon's affable but unassertive former law partner, was to be cut out of foreign policy decisions. To marginalize Defense Secretary Melvin Laird, Kissinger set up a direct line to the Joint Chiefs of Staff, thus undermining the chain of command and the long-held tradition of civilian control of the Pentagon. Nixon and Kissinger also went to extensive lengths to conduct their own foreign policy in secret. Congress, the State Department, and the press were to know as little as possible. The two men even resorted to using their own translators, supplied by foreign officials, so that the State Department bureaucracy wouldn't know what they were doing. (This questionable arrangement might have been attacked by Nixon had it not been of his own devising.) Similarly, Nixon distrusted the CIA, and considered it too soft on the Soviet Union and dominated by "Ivy League intellectuals." Moreover, CIA director Richard Helms, a debonair and well-connected man, was too welcome in the despised Georgetown salons, as were other top CIA officials. In 1973, Nixon acted on his long-nursed resolve to fire Helms, and Helms's successor carried out a purge of CIA personnel.[4]

Nixon and Kissinger's new arrangement would of course make it more difficult for dissenting views to get through to the White House — which was fine with both men — and it would also deny the White House a considerable amount of information and expertise. They were so absorbed with the major world issues that it was hard to get their attention on lesser ones. In the end, Rogers was largely left out in the cold, but Laird, a politically savvy former member of the House Republican leadership, had strong connections on Capitol Hill and was harder to shunt to the sidelines. Laird, who already had doubts about the Vietnam War, had earlier urged a "de-Americanization" policy — which he later replaced with the term "Vietnamization" — and he continually argued for drawing down the number of American troops there. Laird's pressing for disengagement from Vietnam greatly annoyed Kissinger.[5]

Nixon and Kissinger's relationship was complicated and even strange. Though Kissinger often portrayed himself as an equal partner, or even mastermind, to Nixon, in fact he was never Nixon's equal. In Melvin Small's words, "Kissinger played the role of courtier at a very Byzantine court."[6] Kissinger was at first anxious about his relationship with Nixon and about establishing his own high place in the court, but his breakthrough came during Nixon's first foreign trip as president — to Europe in February 1969. On the first night, an elated Nixon invited Kissinger to come by his London hotel suite and asked him to recount how splendid the president's performance that day had been. In a role he was to play many times over the next five years, Kissinger obliged.[7] Nevertheless, the mercurial Kissinger sometimes irritated Nixon with his frequent threats to resign and his fits over Rogers and other possible impediments to his supreme position. At times Nixon considered firing him for insubordination or perceived — and sometimes actual — disloyalty.[8] (Nixon was aware that Kissinger was leaking stories to journalists about how he had saved the day on some foreign policy matter.)

Nixon also retained a certain jealousy of his lionized and socially popular national security adviser. Kissinger relished the high life, attention, and social standing that his office bestowed on him (divorced, he dated movie stars and other beautiful women); the rather dumpy professor who could display considerable charm coined the immortal phrase "Power is the ultimate aphrodisiac." Kissinger was a star in Hollywood in addition to the Georgetown salons. Nixon was at first amused by stories about Kissinger's active social life but later turned envious and then angry about it. His irritation, and attention to details, was demonstrated in a memo Haldeman sent out in 1971 stating that the president wanted a change in the policy — which Kissinger had demanded — of seating the national security adviser next to the most beautiful woman in the room at state dinners.[9] Kissinger was also playing a double game; he tried to stay in good standing with his former Harvard colleagues by assuring them that he was seeking the extrication of the United States from Vietnam, while in the White House he was arguing to Nixon against too rapid a withdrawal from Vietnam.

According to Kissinger's biographer Walter Isaacson, when Nixon took office he had concluded that the United States couldn't win the Vietnam War and was determined to end it quickly.[10] But the North Vietnamese, seeking the unified Vietnam they had been promised in the Geneva Accords of 1954, were more disciplined and determined nationalists than the South. But Nixon and Kissinger worried that a quick retreat would diminish America's standing in the world, and they shared the goal of seeking "peace with honor." In any event, as Stanley Karnow wrote in his definitive book *Vietnam,* "Nixon had no intention of retreating entirely from Vietnam — not, at least, during his presidency."[11]

In their desire to impress the Soviet Union and others that the United States wouldn't walk away from its commitments, they devised their own trap. They sought to buy time, and to provide the shaky and corrupt South Vietnamese government a "decent interval" (Kissinger's term) to stay in power for some time after the war ended. Nixon was loath to be the first American president to lose a war; as a former leading member of the "who lost China" band, he wanted to avoid a similar debate over his Vietnam policy. Kissinger later wrote that the declaration of the goal of "peace with honor" was also a way of appeasing conservatives at home.[12]

Yet Nixon also understood that for political reasons he had to begin to withdraw troops from Vietnam. The result was a contradictory policy. To try to placate critics of the war, Nixon would gradually withdraw U.S. troops from Vietnam, their responsibilities turned over to the South Vietnamese; at the same time, Kissinger would conduct secret negotiations with the North Vietnamese government, bypassing the South Vietnamese regime. But, as Karnow pointed out, if Nixon was withdrawing troops anyway, the North Vietnamese could simply outwait him and prepare to take over as the South Vietnamese government crumbled. There was no real need for them to make concessions.[13]

In July 1969, during a trip to Guam to meet with South Vietnamese leaders and the U.S. military command in Vietnam, Nixon told reporters that he was developing a policy that would connect the commitment of U.S. military aid to other countries with a requirement that those countries provide their own troops. His aides, with their propensity for pronouncing grand concepts, dubbed this the "Nixon Doctrine." The doctrine, aimed really at South Vietnam, was a means of covering the withdrawal with a policy and of assuring others that he wasn't reversing himself in the fight against communism.

Nixon at first believed that the gradual withdrawal of U.S. troops from Vietnam would encourage the North Vietnamese to reduce their own forces in the South and cause them to be more flexible at the Paris negotiations. But the North Vietnamese weren't interested. Nixon and Kissinger also developed the strategy of "linkage," in which relations with the Soviet Union would be affected by its efforts to get the North Vietnamese to negotiate a compromise. Bypassing the State Department, Kissinger established back-channel relations with the Soviet ambassador in Washington, Anatoly Dobrynin. But the Soviets proved unhelpful on Vietnam. So Nixon's early optimism, shared by others in his administration, soon gave way to disappointment and a decision that the war might have to be settled by force — even as the United States gradually withdrew troops. Through Dobrynin, Nixon sent an ultimatum to North Vietnam: if a breakthrough in the negotiations didn't occur by November 1, 1969, he would take "measures of great consequence and force." But the threat was made without a plan for enforcing it.

The threat was one manifestation of Nixon's particular view of how to deal with foreign opponents, which he explained to Haldeman as they were walking along a beach during the 1968 campaign. "I call it the madman theory, Bob. I want the North Vietnamese to believe that I've reached the point where I might do anything to stop the war. We'll just slip to them the word that, For God's sake, you know Nixon is obsessed about communism. We can't restrain him when he's angry — and he has his hand on the nuclear button — and Ho Chi Minh himself will be in Paris in two days begging for peace." Nixon also believed, Haldeman later wrote, that because of his years of thundering against the communist threat, the communists feared him above any other American politician — and that he could end the Vietnam War within a year.[14] The "madman theory," which Kissinger both mocked and bought into, led to the threats, sudden thrusts, and bombing spasms that characterized Nixon's conduct of the war. In later years it was disclosed that in October 1969 Nixon secretly ordered a world-wide nuclear alert, which lasted for a month, to frighten the Soviets into pressing the North Vietnamese to make concessions in the Paris talks. The Strategic Air Command was ordered to fly B-52s, loaded with nuclear weapons, toward the borders of the Soviet Union. The Soviets were aware of the activity at their borders but didn't react. The fact that this alert had happened remained secret for years, and even then received little attention.[15] One danger of the madman theory — of appearing ready to act irrationally — is that the other side might respond with military force. Another problem with the madman theory was that over time it convinced much of the American public that the president was out of control. And another was that it didn't work.

With the November 1, 1969, deadline for progress in the Vietnam peace talks approaching, Kissinger, without telling Laird, set out to devise a plan for a resumption of the bombing of North Vietnam — dropping bombs on Hanoi and mining the harbor at Haiphong. But Laird found out about the planning for the bombing and was strongly opposed, and he argued to Nixon that such a course would be politically disastrous. Kissinger aides opposed the idea as well. Some also argued that Vietnamization was unworkable, that the South Vietnamese would never be able to stand on their own, and that the gradual withdrawal of troops would only encourage North Vietnam to hold fast. Some argued for a deal in which the North Vietnamese and Vietcong be allowed to stay in South Vietnam (this was to happen four years later) and that a coalition government be formed in Saigon. Some even argued, presciently, that no future deal with North Vietnam would be better than one they could reach at that time, and suggested a cease-fire — a policy Nixon and Kissinger would eventually adopt but only after a great deal more carnage.

At the same time, Nixon was under increasing political pressure as more calls were coming from Capitol Hill to hasten the withdrawal. A series of peaceful demonstrations in local communities, called "moratoriums," began on October 15, 1969, and continued over the following several months. Huge crowds turned out in several major cities. A total of 250,000 demonstrators gathered in Washington on October 15. That night, Nixon wrote a note to himself on a yellow legal pad: "Don't get rattled — don't waver — don't react."[16] A couple of days later Kissinger recommended against the bombing attacks on North Vietnam, and Nixon set the idea aside. The November 1 deadline to North Vietnam came and went, but Nixon continued to make threats. And despite the Soviet Union's failure to help resolve the situation, Nixon agreed to an offer from Dobrynin to begin arms-control talks. Nixon's bluff had been called.[17] After feigning indifference to the peace marches, Nixon decided he had to make a major speech in response to the public pressures on him to end the war. On November 3, having backed away from his threats, Nixon gave his famous "great silent majority" speech, calling on those Americans to continue backing him on Vietnam, and pledging what he could not achieve: to make the South Vietnamese forces strong enough to defend themselves and to compromise with the North Vietnamese government provided that it agree to recognize the legitimacy of the South Vietnamese government. The speech was temporarily successful. Nixon also set Spiro Agnew loose at that time to attack liberals and the media as a "small and unelected elite." Television companies and stations were besieged with phone calls from Nixon backers, often immediately following a program and seeming organized, and the pressure did in fact have an impact on news programmers, who became noticeably more timid.

At the end of Nixon's first year in office, as a result of numerous battles and the controversial covert CIA-run "Phoenix" program, which was designed to destroy the Vietcong's rural apparatus in the South and often ended in intensive bombing and the rounding up of innocent peasants and the torture of many, the North Vietnamese forces were weakening and many of the Vietcong were demoralized and had largely left the field.[18] At the same time, the South Vietnamese forces were gaining strength. Some of the North Vietnamese and Vietcong fighters retreated to sanctuaries in Cambodia.

On February 21, 1970, Kissinger began meeting in secret in Paris with North Vietnamese leader Le Duc Tho, separately from the formal peace talks that were taking place elsewhere in the city and bypassing the South Vietnamese government and the U.S. bureaucracy. The problem for Kissinger was that his government was under pressure to resolve the war but Le Duc Tho's wasn't.

By April 1970, Nixon, frustrated by the lack of more progress in the war and the deadlock in the Paris peace talks, was determined to make a show of strength. At the time, Cambodia was beset with internal turmoil: the wavering and somewhat feckless Prince Norodom Sihanouk had been deposed and was replaced by a right-wing military man, Lon Nol, whom Nixon secretly decided to back. The Khmer Rouge, a Cambodian communist guerrilla force trained in North Vietnam, was pushing inward and rival Cambodian groups were brutally murdering each other. Nixon decided to, in his own words, "go for broke" in Cambodia. By several accounts, as he led up to the decision to invade Cambodia, Nixon was in a particularly agitated state. His two Supreme Court nominations had been defeated; war protests were limiting his movements (he was advised that he ought not attend his daughter Julie's graduation from Smith College); and he was spending a lot of time at Camp David with his pugnacious friend Bebe Rebozo and drinking enough that his words were slurred in calls to aides. He had fallen into the habit of watching *Patton* again and again.[19]

By this point, the United States had been conducting "secret" bombing of Cambodia, a neutral country, since March 1969, seeking to destroy North Vietnamese sanctuaries along the border with Vietnam and the elusive headquarters of the communist forces or COSVN (the Vietcong's Central Office for South Vietnam). Secretary of

State Rogers had been opposed to the bombing, and Secretary of Defense Laird was sharply opposed to the secrecy. In May of that year, William Beecher of the *New York Times* revealed the bombing.

The main reason for the secrecy was to avoid inflaming the American public. (Surely, Cambodians were aware of the bombing.) Nixon had gone back and forth for two weeks on the decision to bomb; but when he made the decision to do so, Kissinger, Laird, and Rogers were worried about what they saw as Nixon's impulsiveness. They were concerned as well about the practicality of such bombing in terms of the ongoing diplomacy, and also, for Laird, the possible repercussions on Capitol Hill and in the media.[20] There was little discussion about the morality of bombing a neutral nation; Nixon had made it clear that such considerations didn't interest him. Then, having made the decision in late February to go ahead with the bombing, Nixon, as he was to do several times, met with Rogers and Laird, pretending that the question was still open. The arguing that ensued among his advisers exacerbated Nixon's distaste for listening to internal debates, and, Kissinger wrote later, "reinforced his tendency to exclude the recalcitrants from further deliberations."[21] In fact, Nixon and Kissinger at times showed a certain distaste for, and impatience with, the messiness of democracy — with public opposition blocking their actions and the meddling by the elected members of Congress.

William Beecher's disclosure of the bombing of Cambodia so enraged Nixon and Kissinger that Kissinger approved the wiretapping, without a court order and in the name of "national security," of some of his own aides, whom Nixon had been suspicious of almost from the outset because of their "dovish" leanings. In time, the wiretapping was expanded to include some journalists with access to high officials. According to Isaacson, Kissinger went along with this not only because he shared Nixon's outrage over the leak, but also because he was anxious to show his mettle to Nixon. The Nixon administration's defense of the warrantless wiretaps in the name of national security was later overturned by the Supreme Court. Moreover, the wiretaps picked up political information and even gossip.[22] In time, Nixon, aware that Kissinger himself was leaking to the press, ordered that logs be kept of his calls.

The "secret" bombing, which went on for over a year, wasn't particularly successful:

the North Vietnamese were still operating out of Cambodian sanctuaries and COSVN — the semimythical rudimentary communist headquarters — hadn't been found. Nixon's military commanders in Saigon were urging him to send ground troops into Cambodia, but Laird and Rogers expressed serious doubts about American involvement in a military raid into Cambodia. On April 22, 1970, Nixon, having decided to use ground troops to attack one of the two Cambodian sanctuaries under consideration, met with his National Security Council. Laird and Rogers urged that such action be held off. Unusually, Agnew spoke up, urging that U.S. troops should join in attacks on both Cambodian targets. Otherwise, Agnew insisted, the administration was simply "pussyfooting." An angered Nixon concluded afterward that he couldn't appear less tough than his vice president, and decided on the larger-scale attack — and he excluded Agnew from further NSC meetings.[23] Nixon also concluded that since he was going to take the heat for a raid on one sanctuary, he might as well raid another one. Kissinger was at first ambivalent about the raids into Cambodia, but came to the conclusion that Vietnamization couldn't work if the North Vietnamese could continue to use Cambodia as a conduit for their military efforts, and that attacking only one sanctuary was pointless.[24] Kissinger also realized that Nixon had made up his mind.

On the evening of the NSC meeting about invading Cambodia, Kissinger received a battery of calls from Nixon. After one post-midnight call, Kissinger ordered an aide to return to the White House to plan the Cambodian attack, saying, "Our peerless leader has flipped out." To his aides, Kissinger frequently referred to Nixon as "our drunken friend" and had them listen in on his phone conversations with Nixon so that they could share his dismay at the slurred words and the presidential rambling.[25] The national security adviser also privately described the president of the United States as a "basket case."[26] In his memoirs of his White House years, Kissinger wrote that during this period Nixon was "somewhat overwrought" and "increasingly agitated."[27] Memoirs of some of the other actors and the historical record strongly suggest that Nixon's decisions on Cambodia were affected by his mood.[28] After the decision was made to raid Cambodia, Nixon invited his aides to yet another viewing of *Patton*.

On the night of April 30, in a combative televised address, Nixon announced to the nation a broad "incursion" into Cambodia, and, drawing on his proclivity for pronouncing a false alternative, argued that the United States could not act like a "pitiful helpless giant." To the discomfort of some of his aides, he couched the attack into Cambodia in Churchillian terms, describing it as a struggle against "the forces of totalitarianism and anarchy" and a test of "our will and character." His advisers had also strongly advised him against mentioning the goal of eliminating COSVN, the Vietcong headquarters, since by then it was known to be not a mini-Pentagon but a moving, amorphous command, unlikely to be found. Nevertheless, Nixon set himself up for later embarrassment by saying that among the targets was "the headquarters for the entire Communist military operation in South Vietnam." Nixon, alone in his hideaway office in the Executive Office Building, had written the speech himself in longhand, relying on the pugnacious Patrick Buchanan to do the polishing.[29] The morning after the speech, the president made an impromptu visit to the Pentagon, shouting, with interspersed obscenities, to astonished military briefers, "I want to take out all of those sanctuaries. . . . Knock them all out." Betraying his state of mind, Nixon went on,

"You have to electrify people with bold decisions. Bold decisions make history, like Teddy Roosevelt charging up San Juan Hill." He added, "Let's go blow the hell out of them."[30] As he toured the Pentagon, Nixon, referring to some recent incidents, remarked on "bums . . . blowing up campuses," which was publicly received as an attack on all dissenters.

Following Nixon's April 30 speech announcing the raid into Cambodia, demonstrations erupted on college campuses. On May 4, four students at Kent State University in Ohio were killed by the National Guard. Four of Kissinger's aides resigned in protest. Two hundred and fifty foreign service officers wrote to Rogers protesting the widening of the war. When Nixon learned of this, he called a State Department official and said, "This is the president. I want you to make sure all those sons of bitches are fired first thing in the morning." This was one of Nixon's several orders that were ignored.[31] Members of Congress expressed outrage over the invasion of Cambodian territory.

On the evening of May 8, anticipating the 100,000-person march that was to begin the next day, Nixon made feverish calls to aides and associates and outside advisers like Billy Graham and Thomas Dewey, the former governor of New York. At shortly before five a.m., the heretofore cloistered president, accompanied only by his valet Manolo Sanchez, decided to pay a visit to the Lincoln Memorial, where, for an hour, he awkwardly spoke to students gathered there — about his days as a football player and about his travels — and asked the students whether they liked to surf.[32] From there, he proceeded to the Capitol, where he told a cleaning woman, "My mother was a saint," and instructed her, "You be a saint, too," and then to the Mayflower Hotel to have breakfast with Sanchez. The large demonstrations that ensued in Washington made for a beleaguered White House, from which one could see smoke curling up on Lafayette Park, directly across Pennsylvania Avenue.

The raids on Cambodia, which seemed to stem all too much from Nixon's own frustrations (and perhaps his agitation and drinking), were quite possibly illegal — there was no congressional authorization to invade another country — and in the end not very successful. The communist forces were able to restock the supplies that were destroyed in the attack. COSVN wasn't found; instead, the invading troops came across a cluster of empty huts. The war had been expanded. The raid pushed the North Vietnamese farther inland, and they ended up controlling more Cambodian territory. In 1975, the Lon Nol government fell to the murderous Khmer Rouge, which then slaughtered more than three million Cambodians. The invasion roused Congress to voice more opposition to Nixon's conduct of the war. The day after Nixon announced the invasion of Cambodia, Senator Frank Church of Idaho announced that he would move to stop it, and on June 30 the Senate adopted an amendment by Church and John Sherman Cooper, Republican of Kentucky, that barred the use of funds for U.S. ground forces in Cambodia. This was long noted as the first congressional action to limit the president's powers in wartime. But the amendment, which Nixon threatened to veto, died in the House. A second Cooper-Church amendment, passed on December 22, barred the use of air power over Cambodia, after ground forces had been officially withdrawn.

Since the first Cooper-Church amendment in effect barred the use of U.S. military forces from attacking the Ho Chi Minh trail in the Laotian panhandle, as Nixon and Kissinger sought to do, the mission was turned over to the South Vietnamese. But their attack, which began in early February and was aided by U.S. bombers, ended in a rout. Afterward, on April 7, 1971, Nixon announced in a televised speech, "Tonight I can report that Vietnamization has succeeded."[33]

On June 13, 1971, the *New York Times* began to publish the Pentagon Papers (formally called *History of U.S. Decision-making in Vietnam, 1945–1968*), shortly followed by the *Washington Post.* But Nixon was by now already enraged by leaks; just a month before he had said to Kissinger and Colson as they and other administration figures sailed down the Potomac on the presidential yacht *Sequoia,* "One day we'll get them [leakers] to the ground where we want them. And we'll stick our heels in, step on them hard, and twist . . . step on them, crush them, show them no mercy."[34] (As Isaacson wrote, such evening sails were not an infrequent excursion, with Nixon drinking and demanding that they all stand at attention when passing the American flag at Mount Vernon, a feat that was not easy for everyone.) The next month, after the Supreme Court denied the Nixon administration's petition to stop the publication of the papers, a furious Nixon, egged on by a furious Kissinger, said in a tantrum to his aides, "I want to know who is behind this and I want the most complete investigation that can be done. . . . I want it done whatever the costs."[35] And thus the actions that were to lead to Nixon's being forced to leave office were launched. Haldeman was to write later, "Without the Vietnam War, there would have been no Watergate."[36]

In January 1972, with the presidential election approaching and little progress being made in Paris, Nixon revealed the existence of the secret talks between Kissinger and Le Duc Tho. Nixon had several reasons for feeling frustrated. The South Vietnamese were putting up little resistance to attacks by the North Vietnamese and were in a panicky retreat. Having reduced the number of U.S. troops in Vietnam to 70,000, the president was anxious to have withdrawn many more troops before the Democratic Party's nominating convention that summer. He instructed Kissinger as he was to return to Paris in early May to tell the North Vietnamese, "Settle or else." But the North Vietnamese weren't intimidated, and Kissinger returned empty-handed. Nixon decided that a greater show of force was necessary. Keeping his secretaries of state and defense in the dark, in early May Nixon ordered more extensive bombing of the North, including the Hanoi area, and the mining of the port of Haiphong, as he had contemplated doing earlier. The intense attacks on North Vietnam didn't cause a great public uproar in the United States, largely because troops were coming home, but public opinion continued to turn against the war. Even Vietnam veterans demonstrated against it. In July, the Senate, reacting to public opinion and against Nixon's unilateral and secretive conduct of the war, approved a resolution calling for a total U.S. withdrawal, subject to the release of U.S. prisoners of war held in the North.

In October 1972, the North Vietnamese, having gained substantial territory in South Vietnam and believing that Nixon wanted a settlement before the election — and apparently worried about what Nixon might do once he was reelected — dropped their demand for the immediate removal of the South Vietnamese government of Nguyen Van Thieu and proposed a cease-fire in place. The makeup of the future government in South Vietnam was finessed for the time being. Kissinger was eager to try to wrap up a deal before the election but, contrary to the general belief at the time, Nixon was in fact less interested. His political henchman Charles Colson advised him that a peace agreement before the election would appear to be a political ploy and also that the blue-collar Democrats who supported his war policies might return to their previous political affiliation. Nixon had all along placed less faith in negotiating than Kissinger did, and he became increasingly concerned that Kissinger, in his eagerness for a settlement, might give away too much — and try to get the credit for ending the war. Nixon also felt that he would be in a stronger negotiating situation after, as expected, he defeated the antiwar candidate George McGovern by a large margin. He wrote in his diary, "The enemy then either has to settle or face the consequences of what we could do to them."[37] Besides, Thieu, who hadn't been told about these new terms for a possible settlement, balked when Kissinger went to Saigon to press the agreement on him. Nixon went back and forth on how hard to pressure the Thieu regime to accept the deal — at times reluctant to be seen to be abandoning an ally, at times threatening Thieu with a cut-off of American aid.[38] Nixon decided to keep the whole thing under wraps until after the election. While Thieu and Nixon delayed, in October the

North Vietnamese publicized the terms of the agreement and said that the Nixon administration was trying to sabotage it. Kissinger, for his part, leaked the fact that he had achieved an agreement in principle with Hanoi. An angry Nixon told Colson, "I suppose now everybody's going to say that Kissinger won the election." To reassure the North Vietnamese and to corner Thieu, Kissinger held his first televised press conference and announced, "Peace is at hand."[39] Nixon was further infuriated by the great praise that was being heaped upon his national security adviser by his admirers in the press. Moreover, peace wasn't at hand.

Following his reelection triumph, Nixon once again zigzagged between the ideas of pressing Thieu further and demanding more concessions from the North Vietnamese. But he felt hemmed in by Kissinger's "damn 'Peace is at hand,' " believing that it both hardened the North's position and put pressure on himself to achieve peace.[40] Other White House aides were stoking his suspicions of Kissinger, and while Kissinger was in Paris, Nixon ordered a private check on how many members of Kissinger's staff had supported McGovern.

Nixon and Kissinger decided that either

there would be a deal or there would be more bombing. The fact that there was a fallacy in the logic of bombing the North because of the South's intransigence didn't seem to get much consideration on the part of either man. The outcome was the infamous "Christmas bombing" of North Vietnam, using B-52s on North Vietnamese targets for the first time. The bombing went on for ten days, not including Christmas, with a resulting loss of American prestige throughout much of the world, as well as of American and North Vietnamese lives; there was also a major loss of U.S. military equipment. As the United States ran out of targets and North Vietnam of antiaircraft weaponry, the North Vietnamese agreed to return to the Paris talks and Nixon halted the bombing on December 30. The concessions that the United States got from the North Vietnamese after that were negligible and generally believed not to have justified the costs. Kissinger, who had supported the bombing despite his misgivings, at the end of the year leaked to friendly columnists that he was troubled by the renewed attacks on the North and characterized them as Nixon's decision. Despite Kissinger's denials, Nixon aides who were now keeping track of his calls knew that he had leaked the story. For a while, an infuriated Nixon stopped taking Kissinger's calls and seriously considered firing him as part of a post-election shake-up.[41] And then, on top of all that, Nixon was angry about being paired with Kissinger as *Time*'s Man of the Year. (Kissinger, anticipating this reaction, had begged *Time* to leave himself out.)

In early January 1973, Kissinger and the North Vietnamese reached an agreement that was very close to the one they had tentatively agreed to in October, with the significant exception that Kissinger accepted wording that treated Vietnam as one state. Thieu went along, on the basis of secret promises by Nixon to enforce any violation of the cease-fire — promises that clearly couldn't be fulfilled and weren't revealed to Congress. On January 23, Kissinger initialed the agreement and Nixon announced a cease-fire. He then retreated to the Lincoln Sitting Room, listened to Tchaikovsky, and refused to take calls. At around midnight, perhaps conveying his own mood, he phoned Kissinger to warn him that success is followed by letdown but that he shouldn't be discouraged.[42]

In March 1973, the last American troops were withdrawn from Vietnam and the draft, a strain on the social fabric, was ended. The

Nixon administration had transferred military assets to the South Vietnamese government and, as the North Vietnamese continued to gain ground, Nixon hinted that the United States might intervene again. But the threat was empty; he was powerless to carry it out. In June, Congress — going further than it had in 1970 — passed a resolution cutting off any further funds for U.S. military action in Southeast Asia, including Vietnam, as of August 15. Nixon and Kissinger implored Congress to extend the deadline, but they were refused, and Kissinger later blamed Congress for causing the inevitable unhappy ending to the war. And in November 1973, a frustrated Congress passed (over Nixon's veto) the War Powers Act, which supposedly curbed a president's authority to start a war, but it in fact allowed him to wage one for ninety days without congressional approval. The confusion arose over the fact that the Constitution gave Congress the sole power to declare war and made the president the commander in chief of the armed forces. The War Powers Act was essentially ignored by later presidents.

In the end, Nixon could not achieve true peace in Vietnam before he was forced from office. On April 30, 1975, five years to the day after Nixon had announced the invasion of Cambodia, the North Vietnamese took Saigon. Thieu had fled to Taiwan five days earlier. The hasty departure of U.S. officials and Vietnamese hoping to escape produced the indelible, and humiliating, photographs of desperate South Vietnamese clinging to the skids of American helicopters as they lifted off from the roof of the U.S. embassy. It was left to the new president, Gerald Ford, to announce that the war in Vietnam had finally ended.

An unresolved, and perhaps unresolvable, debate followed over whether the Vietnam War needed to have continued for so long. Some critics have argued that shortly after coming to office, Nixon could have announced that the situation in Vietnam was far worse than he had thought, blamed that on the Democrats, and begun seeking the sort of agreement he ended up with anyway — or simply announced that the United States had fulfilled its commitment to South Vietnam and withdrawn the troops. At the same time, this argument goes, he could have employed tough rhetoric to calm the Right. But instead, Nixon chased a chimera — "peace with honor" — that wouldn't betray his ally, the inept, corrupt South Vietnamese regime, and was supposed to enhance U.S. standing in the world. Critics also argue that the deal that Nixon and Kissinger achieved with the North Vietnamese in 1973 — a cease-fire, a withdrawal of American troops, and leaving the composition of the next South Vietnamese government to a commission — could have been reached as early as 1969. Whether these approaches would have worked cannot be known, but given the outcome and the costs, and of course with the benefit of hindsight, there's a very strong argument that they should have been tried. Or Nixon might have tried for the cease-fire in place much earlier, as some of Kissinger's aides had urged. Or that he should have offered the concession of allowing North Vietnamese troops to remain in the South in 1969 rather than wait until 1972. Since the two architects of the U.S. policy had known all along that "victory" wasn't achievable, they wasted a great deal of blood — in the end the lives of roughly twenty thousand American troops — and treasure in seeking to maintain American pride and standing in the world by pursuing an amorphous "decent interval" and staked the country's reputation on the capacities of an unstable, weak government. In the end, by protracting the war, the Nixon administration lost what it hoped its policy would achieve: the nation's "credibility." And it lowered its moral authority in the world. Nixon inherited a war that was increasingly unpopular and which he had pledged to end. Yes, he did wind it down and the last American troops were withdrawn in March 1973, though the bombing of Cambodia continued, but it ended almost five years after he took office, in part because his policy was unrealistic but in large, immeasurable, part because others — Congress, the press, and, most important, the public — forced his hand.

As the Vietnam War dragged on, Nixon and Kissinger were also laying the groundwork for their greatest triumphs. For all of the attention and energy they spent on Vietnam, and the symbolic importance they attached to the war there, to them Vietnam was essentially a sideshow, fought in large part so that big powers, especially the Soviet Union, wouldn't see the United States as weak, giving up — as a "pitiful, helpless giant." As Nixon and Kissinger demonstrated elsewhere, they weren't really interested in "small," powerless countries. Their apparent callousness about the Vietnam War's great costs, as well as its damage to the fabric of the country and Americans' trust in their government, came about in large part because, in their view, there were greater geopolitical goals at stake. Their big idea was to open or improve U.S. relations with China and the Soviet Union. This was, they believed, the key to global stability and the security and prestige of the United States. They understood that the Vietnam War damaged America's standing in the world and raised questions about its credibility, and they saw the need to reestablish the United States as a great power. They worried that because of their focus on Vietnam, relations with the Soviet Union were not moving forward; moreover, the Soviets were enhancing their nuclear arsenal to near-parity with the United States, and Nixon and Kissinger saw a need to establish better relations with China, an increasingly powerful nation. Moreover, if Nixon and Kissinger were to be seen as great statesmen, they had to perform great acts of statesmanship. Adopting the policy of "realpolitik" meant that Nixon could leave behind his Cold War baggage of "monolithic communism" and deal with the more complex world he now recognized.

As it happened, the Soviet Union and

China, each for its own reasons, were interested in improving relations with the United States. In fact, according to Cold War historian John Lewis Gaddis, in the early 1950s some foreign-policy specialists "were confident that differences between the Russians and the Chinese would eventually arise."[43] Skirmishing on the Sino–Soviet border had begun in 1969, and each side saw the other as a major threat. This gave Nixon an opportunity to "triangulate," to play the two nations off against each other. The Chinese, like the Americans, wanted to counter what they saw as a dangerous Soviet Union. As it happened, both Nixon and Mao Zedong — toward the end of the tumultuous Cultural Revolution — wanted to restore order in their countries. China was losing interest in the Vietnam War and becoming more concerned about threats from the Soviet Union. Mao himself in 1969 had commented to a startled associate, "Richard Nixon is a rightist. . . . I like to deal with rightists. They say what they really think — not like the leftists, who say one thing and mean another." Around the same time Nixon told a startled cabinet that the United States could not allow China to be "smashed" by the Soviet Union.[44] He subsequently informed the

Soviet Union that the United States wouldn't tolerate an attack on China.[45] The Soviet Union, in turn, wanted to raise its standing in the world following its brutal invasion of Czechoslovakia in 1968 to crush its moves toward independence from the Soviet bloc, which had led to a freeze in relations with the United States. So the two communist powers competed to improve relations with the United States, and Nixon, who had perceived this possibility, capitalized on the new state of affairs. This required a subtle balancing act.

Neither the word nor the concept of détente with the Soviet Union originated with Nixon. On the president's first trip to Europe, Charles de Gaulle urged Nixon to exploit the growing tensions between Moscow and China, arguing that the Soviet Union might decide that it couldn't fight both China and the United States and might be ready for a period of rapprochement. De Gaulle said, "To work toward détente is a matter of good sense: if you are not ready to make war, make peace."[46]

There had already been some periods of "thaw" in the relationship between the United States and the Soviet Union; Lyndon Johnson had held a summit meeting with Alexei Kosygin in 1967 and made other attempts to normalize relations between the two nations, including the first steps toward an arms-control agreement through the Strategic Arms Limitation Talks, or SALT. Nixon saw advantages in continuing the efforts at achieving détente and trying to halt the arms race — now entering a new, more dangerous phase — as well as in seeking to offset the enormous drain on national resources caused by the Vietnam War. He wanted to avoid the two nations reaching the kind of precipice they had come to during the 1962 Cuban missile crisis, and, in effect, abandon the brinkmanship of the Eisenhower–Dulles period. Nixon and Kissinger saw an arms-control agreement as part of their larger effort to achieve détente.[47] At the same time, the Soviet Union was also seeking to reduce its military spending, as well as elevate its standing in the world as a superpower on a par with the United States. And both sides were interested in expanding trade between their two nations. Also, some European nations were seeking to reach better relations with the Soviet Union, most notably West Germany, whose chancellor, Willy Brandt, advocated a policy of "Ostpolitik," which aimed at improving relations with East Germany and the Soviet Union. Brandt's overtures annoyed Nixon and Kissinger, and they were determined to preempt them. The situation required deft diplomacy, and an ability to play the Soviet Union and China off each other. No two people were better suited to do that than Nixon and Kissinger. But there were flaws in their thinking: in their belief that playing the two countries off each other in seeking better relations with the United States, they would both be less supportive of North Vietnam; and they overlooked the deepening rift between the Soviets and the Chinese that was already taking place.[48]

Nixon wanted to pursue détente with the Soviets. In the latter part of 1969, he sent the Soviets a signal that he was interested in a summit meeting, even as he was still pressing them, unsuccessfully, to persuade the North Vietnamese to settle the war. Nixon and Kissinger had differing views on how to proceed with Moscow: though the CIA had advised Nixon early on that the Soviets had no real control over the North Vietnamese, Nixon had more confidence than Kissinger did that leaning on the Soviet Union to lean on the North Vietnamese would work. Nixon in fact was prepared to cancel the summit meeting if the Soviets didn't accept this role. Kissinger, for his part, was more interested in pursuing a better relationship with the Soviet Union, regardless of its behavior toward North Vietnam.[49] But once Nixon, despite the Soviets' failure to help out on Vietnam, agreed in the summer of 1969 to resume the SALT talks, and then made overtures for a summit meeting with the Soviets, "linkage" was dead. Lower-level officials were assigned to do the arms-control negotiating while Nixon remained focused on Vietnam and on the great-power relationships. The main issues in the arms talks were the Anti–Ballistic Missile (ABM) system that the Johnson administration had committed to, though in a very limited form, and which Nixon had endorsed in an expanded form in March 1969. The proposed larger ABM system met with great resistance in Congress. It would amount to an escalation of the arms race, and scientists cast great doubt on its efficacy, arguing that it could be overcome by the multiple-warhead missiles, or MIRVs, which, in perhaps the most destabilizing development in the arms race, the United States had begun to manufacture and the Soviets were developing. Unknown at the time, Nixon had his own doubts about the ABM system, but endorsed it in order to have a "bargaining chip" in any upcoming arms-control negotiations.[50] Thus, despite his own well-hidden misgivings, Nixon fought hard to stave off a Senate resolution to ban any ABM deployment — winning the struggle by a narrow margin.

As the Moscow summit remained unconsummated, on July 15, 1971, Nixon astonished the world, and most particularly the Soviet Union, by announcing that he would attend a summit meeting with China in 1972. Thus began the triangulation. As the SALT negotiations continued, Kissinger pushed for an agreement so that it could be signed in a summit meeting in Moscow in 1972. Nixon was less interested in the arms negotiations than was Kissinger, but both wanted the summit meeting to take place. Kissinger distrusted the official arms-control negotiators as too eager for disarmament. So though he knew less about the details of nuclear weapons than they did, and though he was already overextended, Kissinger conducted the real negotiations through his back channel to Ambassador Dobrynin, making big decisions without the advice of the experts — and making big mistakes. (The Joint Chiefs of Staff were also ignored.) Since Nixon wasn't interested in the details of arms control, Kissinger essentially had a free hand. The United States retreated from its earlier insistence that any agreement should be comprehensive, covering offensive as well as defensive weapons, and in the end the SALT agreement did little to change the status quo. The two countries agreed to limit to two the number of ABM systems each country could have (in part because the United States was further ahead on the technology of missile defense, in part because U.S. leaders knew that it would be politically difficult to persuade Congress to expand the system), and it only ostensibly put limits on offensive nuclear systems. It did not limit MIRVs, and, in effect, it allowed the continuation of the arms race. When the principal negotiator, Gerard Smith, upset about the agreement, tried to explain to Nixon some of the problems he found with it, the president replied, "Bullshit."[51] Though a basic agreement on SALT was reached in the spring of 1972, Nixon instructed Kissinger to leave some of the final details for a summit meeting, so that the signing of the agreement could make big news there.

In April 1972, Kissinger made a secret trip to Moscow to prepare for a summit meeting later that spring. True to form, he arrived in Moscow without informing the American ambassador there. (Even Rogers hadn't been told that Kissinger was taking the trip.) During his visit he received feverish instructions from Nixon, via Alexander Haig, the deputy national security adviser, who, to Kissinger's annoyance, was working his way into Nixon's inner circle by being more hard-line than Kissinger and convincing the top White House echelons that he could "handle Henry" — that is, deal with Kissinger's frequent tantrums. The essence of the cables was that Kissinger should "hang tough" on pushing the Soviets to lean on the North Vietnamese — to the exclusion of other issues. At the time, Nixon was once again ensconced with his friend Bebe Rebozo at Camp David. Kissinger, complaining to his staff about Nixon's "idiocies," ignored the instructions.[52]

On May 22, 1972, Nixon arrived in Moscow for his first summit meeting with Soviet leader Leonid Brezhnev. His aides had planned the timing of the trip so that it wouldn't take place so close to the coming presidential election as to appear blatantly political, but close enough to be politically helpful. At the time, the United States was bombing Hanoi and Haiphong, and the Soviets gave Nixon a mixed welcome. But the summit was fruitful. It not only eased relations between the United States and the

Soviet Union, but produced the final SALT agreement and a series of other agreements concerning cooperation on science and technology, as well as a joint space mission. The two sides agreed on a thousand-word document stating "Basic Principles," endorsing "peaceful coexistence" and stating that neither power would try to gain military advantage over the other. In another first, Nixon addressed the Soviet people on television. Upon his return to Washington, he spoke before a joint session of Congress, proclaiming "the end of that era which began in 1945."[53]

Nixon had to work hard to sell the SALT agreement to Congress. He appeased the doves who were complaining that the deal let the arms race continue by pledging that there would be future arms-reduction negotiations; he appeased the hawks who were upset with the very idea of negotiating arms limits with the Soviet Union by pledging that there would be a continuing arms buildup. But in seeking Senate approval of the treaty, which he achieved, Nixon oversold the SALT agreement's benefits and angered promilitary Democrats, such as Senator Henry Jackson of Washington, who did not approve of the administration's dealings with the Soviet Union; Jackson was particularly concerned about its tight limits on Jewish emigration, but he was essentially a hawk on foreign policy and arms control. One result of the overselling of SALT was that it undermined political support for further agreements. Kissinger later wrote, "There was a growing debate over détente, a mounting clamor that in some indefinable way we were being gulled by the Soviets." He went on to argue that détente helped the United States reduce Soviet influence in the Middle East.[54]

Nixon and Brezhnev held two more summits, the first in the summer of 1973 in California, where Brezhnev stayed at Nixon's San Clemente house, and another in June 1974, in Moscow. The results of the next two summits weren't as extensive as those of the first one. Both sides vowed to try later to reach a more comprehensive SALT II treaty, but détente was crumbling and such an agreement wasn't reached during Nixon's presidency. When the San Clemente summit was taking place, the Senate Watergate committee was in the midst of its investigation (in consideration of Nixon's meeting with Brezhnev, it postponed the incriminating testimony of John Dean), and by the time of Nixon's 1974 trip to the Soviet Union there was considerable speculation that the House of Representatives would vote to impeach him. These events distracted Nixon and made it all the more difficult for him to sell his détente policy to the public as well as to numerous politicians — and even to some members of his own administration. As a result, détente was on shaky ground by the time Nixon left office. Powerful anti-Soviet figures on the right charged that Nixon, under pressure to achieve some results, had given away too much.

But despite the parlous political condition Nixon was in, no matter the doubts on the right and left about his conduct of foreign policy, and even though his successor as president was less enthusiastic about it, Nixon's policy of détente with the Soviet Union, flawed as it might have been, had a long-lasting beneficial impact on world history.

Just as Nixon believed that as the old red-baiter he was particularly well suited to bring off better relations with the Soviet Union, he also was convinced that he was the person best suited to open diplomatic relations with China and get away with it politically. He also felt that by warming relations with China, he would have more leverage in his dealings with the Soviet Union. Even before he came to office, Nixon had begun to consider the benefits of opening relations to China; he wrote an article on the subject for *Foreign Affairs* in October 1967. The opening to China was Nixon's vision; he was at first more interested in the idea than Kissinger was.

On his 1969 trip to Europe, Nixon asked de Gaulle to tell the Chinese that he was interested in improving relations. Later that year, he took some steps to encourage better relations with China: easing trade and travel restrictions, ending the Seventh Fleet's patrol of Taiwan, removing nuclear weapons from Okinawa. Nixon and Kissinger began a quiet, elegant pas de deux with China and eagerly sent signals that they wanted to talk. (They cut out the State Department, believing that the traditional-minded bureaucrats would try to slow the process. They also wanted to avoid criticism from conservatives before they pulled off their coup.) There had been off-and-on informal contacts between the United States and China in Warsaw, and these resumed in earnest in early 1970, when the two sides began to discuss a high-level official U.S. trip to China. For a time, the Americans were more interested in a summit than were the Chinese. Nixon continued to send signals. In public, he began to refer to "the People's Republic of China" rather than "Red China." In April 1971, what seemed like a small gesture was a very big thing: the Chinese government invited an American Ping-Pong team, then playing in Japan, to visit China, an event that received considerable press coverage in the United States. Later in April the Chinese informed the administration that they were ready to receive a high-level American official. Nixon, now growing jealous of Kissinger's glowing coverage, toyed with him at first, suggesting other names, but after a while told him that he could make the trip. And so, during a visit to Pakistan in the summer of 1971, Kissinger let it be known that he had "stomach flu" and secretly went to China. Chinese leader Mao Zedong had figured, accurately, that Nixon would very much want to go to China in 1972, an election year. Kissinger pledged to Chinese foreign minister Zhou Enlai that Nixon would visit China before he visited the Soviet Union, and asked that no Democrat be allowed to visit China before Nixon did.

An elated Nixon announced the breakthrough on national television on the evening of July 15. When he asked for television time, almost everyone expected that he would speak about Vietnam — this was an opportune moment for him to be announcing positive news. The economy was dragging and his popularity was sinking; opposition to the Vietnam War was intense; public skepticism about government was growing, especially in the wake of the publication of the Pentagon Papers. As Mao had figured, the White House had been searching for ways to put Nixon on a better footing for the 1972 election. His stunning announcement that he would visit China seemed to boost Nixon's own flagging self-confidence. (He made sure that he, rather than Kissinger, made the announcement.) Unaccustomedly, rather than return to the isolation of his San Clemente home, where he had been staying, after his televised announcement he celebrated with members of his staff, with whom he rarely socialized, at a fine Los Angeles restaurant, ordering an expensive bottle of wine. Nixon had reason to celebrate; the opening to China was perhaps the most imaginative, constructive act of his presidency.

Nixon sent Kissinger a memo instructing him on how to talk about the forthcoming trip to China. It said in part that Kissinger should say, "Nixon is uniquely prepared for this meeting," that among his characteristics were "strong convictions; came up through adversity; at his best in a crisis. Cool. Unflappable."[55]

And so, unlikely as it might have seemed earlier in his career, Richard Nixon went to China on February 1, 1972, staying there for six days. When Nixon met with Mao — a meeting he longed for but hadn't been promised (Mao was ill) — he didn't invite Secretary of State Rogers to join him and used Mao's translator rather than someone from the State Department. And it was a meeting of minds. Each man had studied the other carefully. Nixon, quoting Mao himself, told him, "I know that you are one who sees when an opportunity comes, and then knows that you must seize the hour and seize the day."[56] Mao told Nixon, jokingly, "I voted for you. . . . I am comparatively happy when these people on the right come to power," to which Nixon replied, "Those on the right can do what those on the left talk about." With his sense of occasion, and with some accuracy, Nixon said, "History has brought us together."[57] Mao flattered Nixon, who was more than a little pleased when Mao called *Six Crises* "not a bad book." Nixon's trip, widely watched on American television, was filled with banquets and tourism. Nixon's famous utterance at the Great Wall — "This is a great wall" — became a widespread joke, though it was in the context of several sentences about the greatness of the Chinese people.

The two sides discussed Vietnam. The Chinese, who had previously seen the war as a useful way to bleed the resources of the United States, now worried about a weakened America vis-à-vis the Soviet Union. But they had to be careful not to drive North Vietnam into the arms of their great communist rival. Though the trip marked a dramatic diplomatic turnaround, nothing much concrete arose from it. The main result was the Shanghai Communiqué, in which the two nations agreed that Taiwan is part of China, and the United States agreed to "the ultimate objective of the withdrawal of all U.S. forces and military installations from Taiwan" when Beijing and Taiwan settled their differences. The communiqué, feverishly negotiated by Kissinger without the advice of the State Department, was greeted with great concern by Rogers and his China experts when they learned about it shortly before Nixon was to sign it.[58] Rogers complained that since the communiqué made no mention of the U.S.–Taiwan defense treaty, the United States would be seen as having sold out Taiwan and that conservatives at home would be in an uproar. Nixon and Kissinger were furious at Rogers for interfering — even though he had a point — and Nixon talked about firing him. (Rogers had had to plead even to be included on the trip.) Kissinger tried to clarify the matter at a news conference. On his last evening in China, Nixon, with his penchant for grand claims, said, "This was the week that changed the world." This, too, was much mocked but, in a way, he was right.

Nixon's opening diplomatic relations with China and achieving détente with the Soviet Union were his diplomatic and historic prizes, and they were substantial achievements. He had, after all, inherited the Cold War, a period more dangerous and alarming than it seemed decades later. In changing the order of things, Nixon demonstrated imagination and suppleness. The details may have been ragged, but the results were highly consequential. Détente may have fallen aside in later presidencies, but Nixon was operating in a different time and context. During his presidency, the Soviet Union was a great deal stronger economically, politically, and militarily than it later became, for both internal and external reasons. Nixon moved the world away from the Cold War confrontation, with all its dangers, though it would take more time, and a later president, to end it.

But this wasn't enough to save his presidency.

Nixon's record in the Middle East was more mixed, in part because he was preoccupied with Watergate, in part because Nixon and Kissinger at times simply miscalculated.

Busy as they were with other foreign policy matters, and to give him something to do, Nixon and Kissinger — for a while — delegated dealing with the Middle East to Rogers. Nixon also worried that Kissinger's being Jewish — his "Jew boy" — might cause problems in the region.[59] But still, the White House second-guessed Rogers, and Kissinger, not overly pleased with the accolades Rogers was receiving for trying to attain peace in the area, worked to undermine Rogers's plans.

When Nixon took office, Israel and its Arab neighbors were living under a shaky cease-fire that had been agreed to at the end of the 1967 Six-Day War. As a result of that conflict, Israel occupied land formerly held by Egypt, Syria, and Jordan. Israel sought a peace treaty and offered to return some of the captured land, but the Arab countries said that there would be no peace agreement until Israel returned all of the occupied territory. Nixon and Kissinger, as they were wont to do, saw the situation through the lens of U.S.–Soviet relations, and assumed that the Soviets had more control over the Arab nations' policies than was actually the case.

While Rogers was publicly offering proposals to settle the Middle East issue, Kissinger believed that a long stalemate there would convince the Arab countries that the Soviets weren't being so helpful, and he took private, devious action to make sure that Rogers's ideas weren't implemented. In 1971 the United States warned the new Egyptian president Anwar Sadat that an Egyptian group with close ties to the Soviet Union was planning to overthrow him. After confirming the plot, Sadat, also disturbed at the lack of Soviet support, in the summer of 1972 ordered the Soviet troops out of Egypt. Sadat hoped that such an action would lead the United States to try to persuade Israel to make a deal. This was when Nixon and Kissinger blundered. They failed to take seriously Sadat's warnings in 1972–73 that if the Israelis didn't withdraw from all the Arab land it had occupied since 1967, he would take unilateral military action, and that there would be an embargo on selling oil to the United States. Nixon and Kissinger not only misjudged Sadat's threat, but Nixon also felt too politically weak in 1973 to take on Israel's American supporters. The result, in October 1973, was an attack on Israel by Egypt and Syria and the sixteen-day Yom Kippur War.

Nixon and Kissinger devised a complicated strategy: they wanted Israel to win, as it was likely to, but not by so much that the Arabs felt utterly defeated — thereby inducing both sides to negotiate. The Middle East war was a particularly alarming situation, since the Soviets were helping the Arab states while the United States was helping Israel and no one could be sure where it would all end. As in the case of the invasion of Cambodia, Nixon believed that as long as he was going to be criticized for aiding Israel, "it's got to be the works." He added, "We have to squeeze the Israelis when this is over, and the Russians have to know it. . . . We have to squeeze them goddamn hard." He also asked Kissinger to remind him how tough he had been on the matter of Cambodia.[60] And then there was a very strange set of events. When the Middle East fighting persisted after a cease-fire, apparently at Israel's instigation, the Soviets on October 24 implied — but didn't overtly threaten — that they would intervene with troops to enforce the cease-fire. Nixon was by that time distraught over calls for his impeachment following the Saturday Night Massacre four nights earlier — and largely remained secluded in the White House residence.

Kissinger was by now both secretary of state and national security adviser; as part of the postelection shake-up in 1972, Nixon had decided that Rogers had to go. Rogers, however, like others, demanded that his old friend Nixon tell him himself that he was being fired and insisted to Nixon that his departure should not look like a "victory for Kissinger" just after the election, and so Rogers was allowed to stay on for a few more months. This arrangement infuriated Kissinger, who was unaware that Nixon was thinking about getting rid of him as well.[61] Kissinger was sworn in as secretary of state in late September 1973, while retaining his White House post.

In response to the ominous Soviet message on October 24, late that night an agitated Kissinger began a series of meetings with other advisers, but without the secluded Nixon; just before midnight the group ultimately agreed that a strong signal had to be sent to the Soviets. And so the president's aides — without informing the president, whom they considered not in a condition to make such an important decision — ordered a worldwide U.S. nuclear and military alert. U.S. air, ground, and sea forces around the world were put in a state of readiness. Nixon didn't learn about it until the next morning.[62] Nixon's aides later insisted that the president had been participating in the decision from the residence, and Nixon, engaging in a bit of fantasy himself, instructed Kissinger to call in major journalists to tell them that Nixon had played a key role in the decision, adding, "Who saved Israel? Would anybody else have saved it? You have to tell them that." The news of the alert, coming as it did just a few days after the Saturday Night Massacre, led many Americans to wonder if this crisis was real, and many believed that their president was once again out of control. Also, on the night of October 20, Saudi Arabia had announced an embargo on oil to the United States, and other Middle East nations shortly followed (as Sadat had warned). As if Nixon didn't have enough problems, the oil embargo resulted in serious U.S. gasoline shortages throughout the winter and into the spring of 1974.

Three days after the alert, Nixon told a press conference that there had been a "real crisis," and that the Soviets had provoked the "most difficult crisis we have had since the Cuban confrontation of 1962." In private, Nixon in fact often spoke enviously of Kennedy's management of the Cuban Missile Crisis as a display of presidential strength.

The alert and the Soviet failure to intervene convinced Middle East countries that only the United States could affect matters in the region. Another cease-fire was reached and then Kissinger embarked upon his famous "shuttle diplomacy," hopping among the former combatant states to, "step-by-step," achieve military disengagements among Israel and Egypt and Syria. He achieved them toward the end of May 1974 and was hailed as "Super K." Nixon, envious of the glory that was accruing to Kissinger, meddled a couple of times but was essentially irrelevant to the Middle East process. Yet two weeks after Kissinger's triumph, Nixon visited all three countries involved — Syria, Egypt, and Israel — claiming another "first" when he arrived in Syria. Egypt and Syria reopened diplomatic relations with the United States. But even if

Nixon could enjoy the positive developments in the Middle East, his satisfaction was limited by the fact that his presidency was now in dire trouble.

Other aspects of the Nixon–Kissinger foreign policy were problematic. Partly because they were preoccupied with other issues, particularly because they were focused on bettering relations with the Soviet Union and China, and partly because of their penchant for realpolitik, they made several missteps. And they continued to see some situations as part of a global plot by the Soviet Union. To help Iran, then a covert ally of Israel, to keep peace in the Middle East, and because it was a major supplier of oil to the United States, Nixon and Kissinger permitted the Shah of Iran to buy an unprecedented amount of U.S. weapons — over the objections of the Defense and State Departments, the latter arguing that the domestic situation in Iran was too unstable. The inflow of the arms was believed by many observers to have caused the Shah to tighten the reins and ignore the needs of his own people. In turn this led to his overthrow in 1979 and brought to power a regime highly hostile to the United States. Also at the urging of the Shah, who wanted to harass the Iraqis, the Nixon administration encouraged the Kurds in northern Iraq to rebel against Saddam Hussein's regime, and, despite the misgivings of the State Department and the CIA, sent them funds to do so — and then abandoned them when the Shah reached an accommodation with Iraq, leaving the Kurds subject to brutal retaliation by Saddam.[63]

In Chile, Nixon and Kissinger were determined to oust Salvador Allende, an avowed Marxist who was democratically elected president in 1970. The administration, through the CIA and large corporations with business interests there, worked to undermine the Chilean economy and encouraged a military coup. The CIA also aided a right-wing band that kidnapped and killed General René Schneider, who was opposed to a military coup. The successful coup on September 11, 1973, in which Allende was killed, led to the brutal, murderous regime of General Augusto Pinochet. Though the United States played no direct role in the coup itself and Allende had already stirred domestic opposition, the Nixon administration helped create the conditions for the coup and its meddling in Chile besmirched its reputation.

During the war between India and Pakistan in 1971, the United States tilted toward the repressive Pakistan because Pakistan was serving as a conduit in Nixon and Kissinger's preparations to deal with China and because Nixon disliked Indian prime minister Indira Gandhi, who he felt had snubbed him. Kissinger wrote that Gandhi's haughty attitude "brought out all of Nixon's latent insecurities."[64] Without telling the secretaries of state or defense — or the public — Nixon ordered a naval task force to the Bay of Bengal to threaten the Indians; the task force arrived there one day after India and Pakistan had reached a tentative peace agreement.

Nixon and Kissinger weren't interested in Africa because it played no role in their great power politics. Nixon told Kissinger, "Henry, let's leave the niggers to Bill [Rogers]," and both men shared racist remarks.[65] Despite Nixon's travels and self-promotion as a world statesman, European leaders other than de Gaulle were largely ignored.

In sum, Nixon and Kissinger's conduct of foreign policy was a curious combination of large, long-sighted achievements and short-sighted blunders — one of them, Vietnam, a tragic one. Some historians diminish their achievements, saying that Nixon and Kissinger inherited situations conducive to great power rearrangements. But their skilled diplomacy in handling those situations overshadows the issue of their origins. Ironically, Nixon benefited from the political context that he had set with his earlier anticommunist activism. As president, he was able to see beyond the threat of "communist world domination" that had driven so much U.S. foreign policy making, and his own prepresidential rhetoric, and at the same time he fell into some traps that his partially clinging to that worldview presented. The Nixon–Kissinger foreign policy was both enlightened and cynical. In their pursuit of realpolitik, and their ignoring the expertise in other parts of the government, and even keeping many of their policies secret, they made several costly mistakes. For both men, Russia and China were the center of their policy universe; everything else, including Vietnam, came within that context. But though the likes of Vietnam and Chile were "small" countries, Vietnam was of course about more than that: Nixon didn't want to lose a war. Their conduct of the Vietnam War led to an unprecedented mistrust of government on the part of a large segment of the American people. Combined with Nixon's suspiciousness, paranoia, and vindictive streak, it also led to his downfall.

6
WATERGATE

The extraordinary set of events that came
to be called Watergate — named for the
building complex where on June 17, 1972,
a team of burglars with ties to the White
House broke into the headquarters of the
Democratic National Committee and cul-
minating in Nixon's becoming the first
president to be forced to leave office — has
often been described as the unraveling of a
criminal conspiracy. But while crimes were
committed in the case of the Watergate
break-in, and in the subsequent cover-up of
how the burglars were financed and their
connections to the White House, these
bizarre developments were even more than
that: they represented a constitutional crisis.
They raised the questions of whether the
president was subject to the law and the
courts; whether the executive branch, in
particular the White House, was account-
able to the other branches of government;

whether Congress would assert itself against a president who held himself above the law. Though, looking back, the unraveling of the cover-up seems inevitable, it didn't appear so at the time. The fact that Richard Nixon was driven from the presidency, that "the system worked," became such a settled part of American history that it has been largely overlooked that this outcome was far from certain. The Watergate era also had its comic moments as a result of the absurdities that were exposed and the bizarre figures that were involved; the mixture of the menacing and the ridiculous put the country through an array of contradictory emotions. Most after-the-fact histories don't convey that for a great many Americans this was a period of fear and tension, a wild ride through history. A place-name became a metaphor, like Waterloo. The public was intensely engaged, not only because the events of the Watergate era were so astonishing, and often frightening, but also because Nixon, with his self-absorption, outbursts, and emotion-ridden talking about them, made this his last and greatest crisis, and he imposed his own agony on the nation.

A couple of weeks after the Pentagon Papers were published in June 1971, John Ehrlichman, following Nixon's orders, established the Special Investigations Unit, or the "plumbers," in the White House to stop such leaks of classified documents. Worried that leaks could undermine his and Kissinger's largely secret international maneuvering, that the Pentagon Papers themselves could undermine the legitimacy of the Vietnam War, and now all the more exercised about the press, Nixon told his aides he wanted a full investigation "whatever the cost," and they took him at his word. The plumbers outfit wasn't hidden away. It was given Room 16 of the Executive Office Building, next to the White House; a sign on the door even said "Plumbers." But their efforts went well beyond ferreting out and stopping leaks.

The plumbers unit was just one manifestation of Nixon's determination to destroy those he considered his enemies. ("Crush them" was a familiar Nixon phrase.) Guided by his paranoia, Nixon's "enemies" fell into several categories: real and potential political opponents; elements in the society — the media, intellectuals, well-bred members of the "elites"; the countercultural "hippies"; and others who protested his Vietnam War policy. He believed that all of these forces were out to "get him" — and he now had the means to retaliate. He made no distinction between opponents and enemies; opponents, political or otherwise, were also to be crushed. Despite Nixon's great political success, he was still harboring and animated by his long-nursed anger and resentments, his lifelong feeling that people of greater means and in more secure positions were looking down on him. His self-description had long been that he was a "fighter," and now he had the power to harass, undermine, or even destroy those who were, or who he thought were, out to destroy him. After all, throughout his political career he had shown a willingness to go beyond the norms of political combat, and he had gotten away with it — even risen by it.

The plumbers' first order of business was to get damaging information on Daniel Ellsberg, the former Pentagon aide who, besides having leaked the Pentagon Papers, was everything Nixon loathed: a liberal intellectual with a Ph.D. from Harvard, an antiwar activist, and a Jew. The leaders of the plumbers unit were E. Howard Hunt and G. Gordon Liddy, neither one the sort of person to serve in a White House. Hunt, a former CIA agent and participant in the Bay of Pigs fiasco, whom special counsel Charles Colson had recommended to chief of staff H. R. Haldeman in July 1971, was now a White House "consultant." Colson had spoken to Hunt about getting information on Ellsberg so that they could "go down the line to nail the guy cold."[1] Hunt was a character out of his own adventure novels: dashing and daring. He donned a CIA-supplied red wig and voice-altering machine when he went to see Dita Beard, a lobbyist for ITT, the huge telecommunications company, during an investigation of its four-hundred-thousand-dollar donation to Nixon's reelection campaign. Liddy, a former FBI agent, had worked in Nixon's campaign and then the Treasury Department, but in June 1971, as the plumbers' outfit was being built, he was abruptly transferred to the White House and placed on the staff of the Domestic Council. The erratic Liddy often carried a gun and could confuse a suggestion to "go after" a Nixon "enemy" as an order to kill him. (He shot out a light while spying on McGovern's headquarters.)[2] The plumbers were put in the charge of Egil ("Bud") Krogh, an earnest young man and member of Ehrlichman's domestic policy staff. Krogh, a former Seattle attorney and protégé of Ehrlichman, was from all appearances the kind of clean-cut, solemn young man who wouldn't do anything wrong. Nixon instructed Ehrlichman to urge the plumbers to read *Six Crises,* especially the chapter on Alger Hiss, in which Nixon said he acted to stop "Communist conspiracy within the United States."[3]

The figures caught up in this drama — from the plumbers to the president's top advisers — acted on a combination of explicit orders from the president, or what his aides thought the president wanted, or what the lower-level operatives thought the president or his aides wanted. In the end, these distinctions didn't matter. All of the actions stemmed from how Richard Nixon chose to use his presidential powers to combat his "enemies."

The seeds for Watergate were planted early in the Nixon presidency and the Watergate break-in was almost a natural progression from some extraordinary steps Nixon took shortly after the outset of his presidency. In February 1969, Nixon told his staff that he wanted private political funds to be used to carry out secret White House intelligence operations, and the next month he approved a plan by Ehrlichman for around-the-clock monitoring of Senator Edward M. Kennedy, a presumed opponent in 1972. Ehrlichman hired Jack Caulfield, a former New York police detective, to run intelligence operations for the White House and who, at his insistence, was put on the White House payroll. Ehrlichman also hired Tony Ulasewicz, another former New York policeman, who was paid from a secret fund being managed by Nixon's personal attorney in California, Herbert Kalmbach.[4] (Ulasewicz was to become the courier for money from Kalmbach to pay off the Watergate burglars, and also one of the most colorful figures in the Watergate episode.) Nixon thus set in motion the use of private funds for political purposes (which had gotten him in trouble before) and an off-the-books intelligence operation to gather information on enemies and take actions against them. This was to be a deadly combination.

When a car driven by Kennedy veered off a bridge on Chappaquiddick, a small island off Martha's Vineyard, Massachusetts, on July 18, 1969, resulting in the drowning of Mary Jo Kopechne, a young woman who had worked for the Kennedys, Ehrlichman sent Caulfield and Ulasewicz to Martha's Vineyard to investigate, posing as journalists.[5] (Reflecting Nixon's fixation on the Kennedys, Charles Colson, Nixon's resident tough guy, had Hunt forge a diplomatic cable purporting to link John F. Kennedy directly with the assassination in 1963 of South Vietnamese president Ngo Dinh Diem, to be released to a news magazine.)

In 1970, his second year in office, Nixon first encouraged and then approved a plan drawn up by White House aide Tom Charles Huston to use the combined resources of several investigative agencies for a program that included breaking and entering, electronic surveillance, and mail covers (a surveillance technique in which the outside of personal mail and postcards are copied in order to track an individual's correspondence — a practice, like wiretapping, restricted by law). After even FBI director J. Edgar Hoover, himself no great civil libertarian, objected, Nixon claimed that the "Huston plan" had been "rescinded." But Huston told a House subcommittee in 1972 that the plan had never been formally canceled. Parts of it were incorporated into the plumbers operation. Nothing like this had ever happened before. As it turned out, the plumbers were not very competent; their missions were usually botched. But the comic aspect of their bumbling didn't make the concept of such an operation less menacing.

Four days after the Pentagon Papers were published in June 1971, and even before the plumbers unit was fully established, Nixon urged his aides to arrange for the firebombing of the Brookings Institution, a liberal-leaning think tank in Washington where some former aides to President Lyndon Johnson had offices. He believed that two former Defense Department aides, Leslie Gelb (who had directed the Pentagon Papers project) and Morton Halperin (who had also served for a while on Kissinger's NSC staff), had parts of the Pentagon Papers that Ellsberg hadn't released. Nixon thought that these additional parts of the report might be embarrassing and could be used to blackmail him. According to a tape of a June 17, 1971, conversation with Kissinger and Haldeman, Nixon, referring to the supposedly rescinded Huston plan that included break-ins, told Haldeman, "I want it implemented. . . . Goddammit, get in and get those files. Blow the safe and get it." As a result, Colson devised a plan to start a fire in the Brookings headquarters and seize papers during the confusion caused by the arrival of fire trucks. The plan was thwarted by other White House aides. In fact, Gelb didn't have a safe, and neither Gelb nor Halperin possessed classified documents — at home or at their office — and none of the Brookings fellows had safes. (Ulasewicz had cased Brookings.)[6]

Later that summer, Colson, who took great pride in his ruthlessness and was eager to get damaging information on Ellsberg, presented Ehrlichman with a "game plan" to carry out the president's instructions to his staff to "crush" leakers, and Ehrlichman approved "Hunt/Liddy Special Project #1." Hunt and Liddy's plan was to break into the office of Ellsberg's psychiatrist, Dr. Lewis Fielding, in Los Angeles, and Hunt recruited four Cuban émigrés who had been involved in John F. Kennedy's failed Bay of Pigs operation to carry it out. Hunt and Liddy first cased Dr. Fielding's office and took pictures of it, and then supervised their team from a distance. The break-in, a blatant violation of the Fourth Amendment's protection against unreasonable searches and seizures of one's personal property, yielded nothing (the burglars couldn't find any files, much less one on Ellsberg), but that didn't discourage the plumbers' supervisors from ordering up further operations. Ehrlichman later claimed that Nixon had approved the Fielding raid.[7] The break-in went undetected for a long time, and didn't become publicly known until March 1973, during Ellsberg's trial for unlawful possession and disclosure of classified material, when the Justice Department felt compelled to disclose it, over Nixon's objections, to the judge in the case. Upon receiving the information, the judge, William Matthew Byrne Jr., suspended the trial. What Nixon and most of the White House staff in all their frenzy didn't know was that Ellsberg had been given access to the Pentagon Papers stored at the Rand Corporation so that he could do a top-secret study for Kissinger.[8] (Kissinger knew and, according to Haldeman, got the president very worked up over the leak.)[9]

The Nixon White House was a nest of activities, most of them illegal, against Nixon's "enemies," and of presidential aides with no sense of limits. The wiretapping without a court order of Kissinger's aides had begun in 1969 and lasted until June 1972, when the Supreme Court unanimously ruled that they were unconstitutional. (Nixon said later that they were "legal at the time.")[10] In May 1971, during the large antiwar demonstration in Washington, Haldeman told Nixon that Colson would use his connections with the Teamsters Union to hire some "thugs" to beat up the protesters. Nixon replied, "Go in and knock their heads off."[11] Thus the Nixon White House had its own "bully boys," its own ruffians, to physically assault opponents of his conduct of the war. This, too, was without precedent. In the late summer of 1971, White House counsel John Dean prepared a plan for an "enemies list" and using the instruments of government, such as the Internal Revenue Service, against them. The idea, Dean said, was "to use the available federal machinery to screw our political enemies." Earlier, Huston had arranged for the IRS to set up a unit, the Special Services Staff, or, chillingly, the SSS, to investigate dissident and leftist groups; by September 1970, the SSS had gathered information on four thousand people and one thousand institutions. Intelligence units in the Justice Department, the military, and the Secret Service were also enlisted in the effort.[12] What all this yielded is unknown — Nixon and his aides felt that the IRS was too unresponsive — but the effort was another reflection of the Nixon White House's mentality.

The following year, Colson provided the first twenty names for the White House's enemies list — Senator Edmund Muskie's chief fund-raiser was at the top — and it included the journalist Daniel Schorr and the actor Paul Newman, who was engaged in antiwar activities. As Dean and other Nixon aides added names, the list grew to two hundred and included other journalists, university presidents, and nonprofit institutions as well as political activists and contributors to the Democratic Party. At the time, some people jokingly considered it a badge of honor to be on the enemies list, but the very idea of using governmental powers to damage real and perceived opponents was, and remains, disturbing.

The Nixon White House's first priority for the 1972 reelection effort was to derail Muskie's candidacy for the Democratic presidential nomination. In 1971, Nixon and his advisers concluded that Senator George McGovern would be the weakest Democratic candidate in 1972 because, in Pat Buchanan's words, he could be portrayed as a "left-wing radical," and they set out to undermine the other possible candidates, particularly Muskie, the statuesque Maine senator, who was leading Nixon in the polls. The Committee to Reelect the President (CRP, but better known as CREEP), now headed by former attorney general John Mitchell, hired Donald Segretti, a former classmate of some Nixon aides, who specialized in political tricks, for the specific purpose of undermining the Democratic Party's nominating process. Segretti, often described to the public as a lone "prankster," operated with a team of twenty-eight agents in seventeen states. They disrupted Democratic Party events by ostensibly jokey actions such as sending in pizzas to a Democratic rally and dropping white mice at a Muskie press conference with ribbons on the tails reading, "Muskie is a rat fink," but they also engaged in more sinister actions such as forging documents, canceling Democratic candidates' events, and leaking false and libelous information on opponents. Campaign documents disappeared from Muskie's office and his campaign manager's files were ransacked.[13] CREEP even managed to place one of its own as Muskie's driver.[14] In 1972, McGovern's presidential campaign was spied upon. That same year White House counsel John Dean demanded Internal Revenue Service investigations of 490 staff members of and contributors to McGovern's campaign. The concept of the party in power trying to disrupt and undermine the opposing party is a serious matter; it's a step on the way to fascism.

Against this backdrop, the Watergate

break-in was just another in a series of projects to help Nixon "get the goods" on his opponents and try to destroy them — almost routine by now. It was part of a project, called Gemstone, which was drawn up by Liddy, now a counsel to CREEP, and approved by Mitchell in March 1972. Gemstone involved electronic bugging and photographing or stealing documents. The famous break-in was actually the second of two — and, according to Eugenio Martinez, one of the burglars, the first one itself followed two failed attempts by Liddy, Hunt, and the Cubans to get into the Democratic National Committee's headquarters in the Watergate office building; the burglars were stymied by locked doors until then, so one of them returned to Miami to retrieve his more sophisticated tools for such efforts.[15] Then, over the following Memorial Day weekend, the plumbers succeeded in breaking into the committee's headquarters, placed taps on two phones, one of them that of DNC chairman Lawrence O'Brien, and photographed documents. But the tap on O'Brien's phone didn't work, and a displeased Mitchell complained to Liddy that what they had gathered was "junk." Liddy told Mitchell he'd "take care of" the problem. So the plumbers — the same four

Cubans plus James McCord, an electronics expert, also a former CIA agent now handling "security" for CREEP — returned to the Watergate to fix the tap.[16] The burglars were wearing surgical gloves and carrying telephone-bugging devices, cans of mace, and $2,400 in cash, including new one-hundred-dollar bills. Liddy and Hunt supervised the burglars' operation from a Howard Johnson motel across from the DNC's headquarters. But this time the burglars were more careless than before, and from the moment the clumsy plumbers were caught by the proverbial night watchman — did they not consider there would be one? — Nixon was engulfed by his obsessions. Now he had to make sure that investigators didn't learn of the White House connections to the break-ins of Dr. Fielding's office as well as the Watergate.

There have been various theories about the purpose of the Watergate break-in — finding out about an alleged call-girl ring involving a DNC aide, or convoluted arrangements between Nixon and the junta that had overthrown the Greek government in 1967, or some sort of CIA setup — but given the pattern of the Nixon White House's activities against the president's "enemies," by far the most likely explanation is that their mission was to "get the goods" on O'Brien, on whom Nixon was fixated — just as they had attempted to "get the goods" on Ellsberg. Nixon had already called for an IRS audit of O'Brien, and, according to later testimony by Mitchell's deputy Jeb Stuart Magruder, Colson had told CREEP officials that the White House particularly needed information on O'Brien.[17] A former top aide to John F. Kennedy, O'Brien not only headed the Democratic Party but he also had worked for Howard Hughes. Nixon particularly resented that he had been vilified for his brother's having accepted money from Hughes, while the fact that O'Brien had worked for Hughes hadn't become publicly known.[18] (It's also possible that Nixon wanted to find out what O'Brien knew about his own connections to Hughes.) Given the proclivities of Nixon and his top aides, they simply may have wanted to know what the chairman of the opposition party was doing. Within a few days of the botched burglary, officials at CREEP began to shred incriminating documents; Mitchell told them to "have a good fire."[19]

What began as an odd police story in the *Washington Post* on June 19 — why had people broken into the Democratic Party's headquarters? — evolved into a national scandal as the press, led by the *Post*'s Bob Woodward and Carl Bernstein, competed to get to the bottom of it. Press secretary Ron Ziegler famously dismissed the Watergate break-in as a "third-rate burglary." At the same time, because the break-in might have involved a violation of federal communications statutes, the local police called in the FBI and federal attorneys — the Criminal Division of the Justice Department and the U.S. Attorney's office for the District of Columbia — began their own investigation of the Watergate break-in. The burglars' connection to the White House was quickly discovered by the federal investigators through a notation "WH" in McCord's address book and a check signed by Hunt.

Nixon returned to Washington from Key Biscayne on June 20, three days after the burglary, and that evening Haldeman briefed him on the involvement of Hunt and Liddy and their relationship to CREEP, as well as Howard Hunt's connection to Colson. Haldeman assured Nixon that Hunt was "in the process of disappearing." Haldeman also remarked, of the burglars, that "they were a pretty competent bunch of people, and they've been doing other things very well, apparently." With striking presentiment, Nixon told Haldeman, who was one of the very few White House aides who knew that a taping system had been installed in the Oval Office, "This Oval Office business [the taping system] complicates things all over." A portion of the tape of this particular meeting — eighteen and a half minutes — was later erased, most probably by Nixon himself.

The following day, Haldeman, speaking about Hunt and his group, advised Nixon, "The problem is that there are all kinds of other involvements" — left unmentioned were the previous break-ins — and that Hunt "was working on a lot of stuff." Haldeman also told Nixon that Liddy was "a little bit nuts." They discussed a suggestion by Mitchell that the FBI be "turned off."[20] And thus the cover-up began.

In meetings over the next few days, an obviously worried Nixon discussed with Haldeman and Colson various ideas about how to handle the situation. And then on June 23 came the fateful discussion in which Nixon and Haldeman expressed their concern that the FBI was "out of control"; it was beginning to trace the source of the money, drawn from a Miami bank, to pay the burglars. So Nixon approved Haldeman's suggestion that they should act on Mitchell's idea that the top officials of the CIA should be instructed to tell the acting FBI director, L. Patrick Gray, to "stay the hell out of this," on the grounds that it would expose sensitive CIA activities. Now Nixon was in very deep.

Later in the summer of 1972, Woodward and Bernstein reported that a cashier's check worth twenty-five thousand dollars intended for the president's reelection campaign had ended up in the bank account of one of the Watergate burglars. Material from Hunt's White House safe, including a report on Chappaquiddick (and the doctored cable), had been turned over to Ehrlichman, who ordered John Dean, the White House counsel, to "deep-six" them, but instead Dean turned them over to Gray. That's how people in the supposedly most revered office in the land talked — like the thugs they turned out to be. (Also found in Hunt's office by the FBI were a Colt revolver, four antennas, six jack wires, a portable transmitter, folders containing material on Ellsberg and the Pentagon Papers, records of his hours working in the pay of the White House, and "Press Contacts.")[21] Shortly afterward, the *Post* reported that even while serving as attorney general, Mitchell had controlled a slush fund to pay for intelligence operations against the Democrats. It later became a commonplace that Nixon's problem wasn't the crime but the cover-up. But that represented less a principle than a statement about Congress's reluctance to proceed against the president. The numerous crimes and misuses of executive power to harass and destroy political opponents and "enemies" seemed reason enough for removing a president, but at the time the idea of doing so was extraordinary and had only one precedent: the impeachment of Andrew Johnson, ostensibly for his removal of the secretary of war, Edwin Stanton, in violation of an act of Congress, which was tinged by post–Civil War bitterness. Johnson's removal from office failed in the Senate by one vote.

The cover-up lasted ten months (during which, of course, Nixon was overwhelmingly reelected to office). But it began to crumble as the prosecution by the U.S. Attorney's office pushed on. On September 15, 1972, the Watergate burglars — the Cubans, Hunt, Liddy, and McCord — were indicted by a grand jury. Nixon took increasingly desperate steps to keep the whole matter from reaching him. But the cover-up truly started to unravel shortly before the Watergate burglars were to be sentenced on March 23, 1973, by Federal District Judge John J. Sirica, known as "maximum John" for his harsh sentencing. On March 20, James McCord sent Sirica a letter (which Nixon was aware of), saying that the burglars had been pressured to remain silent, that the operation hadn't been carried out by the CIA but by other government officials, and that perjury had been committed. Sirica imposed heavy sentences on the other Watergate burglars. (McCord was later given a lighter sentence.) Though sometimes he tried to slough it off to others, Nixon was aware of the danger he was in.[22] He later wrote in his memoirs that at this point he realized that "Vietnam had found its successor."[23]

On March 21, two days before the sentencing, John Dean, whom Nixon had made a show of asking to investigate the break-in, told Nixon, "We have a cancer within, close to the presidency, that is growing daily." Dean told Nixon that the cover-up was failing, and that the Watergate burglars were blackmailing them for more money. When Dean told Nixon that he would need a million dollars in hush money over two years, the president replied that the money could be gotten in cash — "I know where it can be gotten. . . . I mean it's easy, it could be done."

There was another aspect of this period that, as it was gradually exposed, damaged Nixon's standing. The Watergate events took place amid a strong stench of corruption, which became part of the story. Not only were there very large contributions from individuals, but also huge, illegal corporate contributions given to Nixon's reelection campaign. Some of these funds were used to pay off the Watergate burglars. Ambassadorships were blatantly sold: on June 23, 1971, Nixon told Haldeman that "anybody that wants to be an ambassador wants to pay at least $250,000."[24] Huge sums of corporate contributions that flowed into the Nixon reelection effort, headed by Mitchell, appeared to be the result of a systematic shakedown scheme. Sometimes these contributions appeared to be linked to Nixon administration actions favorable to these interests. The trucking industry gave the Nixon reelection campaign more than six hundred thousand dollars while it was fighting an unfavorable government proposal; the Associated Milk Producers pledged two million dollars two weeks before Nixon imposed a quota on some imported dairy products. Murray Chotiner, now in private law practice, and Howard Hunt headed one of the dummy committees to handle the milk money. In 1969 and 1970, Howard Hughes gave Bebe Rebozo one hundred thousand dollars, money that was apparently used for personal items (platinum and diamond earrings for Pat) and to pay off the burglars; the disclosure of this was particularly embarrassing to Nixon because of the large, controversial loan Hughes had also made to Nixon's brother Donald in 1956. The Hughes money was later replaced in order to present it to the Senate committee investigating Watergate as not having been spent. (In December 1973, an attorney for Hughes appeared before a closed meeting of the committee and startled its members when he dumped one hundred thousand dollars in cash from a suitcase and said, "Here's the goddam money." Actually, there were $101,000 in bills and clear signs that the original cash had been used and replaced.)[25] Among the corporations that ultimately pled guilty to making illegal contributions to Nixon's reelection campaign were American Airlines, the Goodyear Tire & Rubber Company, and the Minnesota Mining & Manufacturing Company.

During the Senate Watergate hearings in

May 1973, it was disclosed that Nixon's attorney Herbert Kalmbach had raised at least $210,000 the previous summer for the Watergate defendants or their attorneys. During that same period, the White House was forced by press accounts to disclose Bebe Rebozo's and Robert Abplanalp's roles in helping Nixon buy his homes in Key Biscayne and San Clemente, and in paying for improvements on his property. The disclosures provoked widespread astonishment that the subject of Nixon benefiting from private contributions was back. In late May 1973, it was disclosed that Abplanalp had received a federal bank charter after he bought the land for the Nixons' California house. The following October, a House subcommittee found that $2,000 in government funds was spent for a black-and-white terrazzo shuffleboard court and $11,500 was spent for a redwood, rather than a wire-mesh, fence for the San Clemente home.[26]

In the spring of 1973, the figures around Nixon began to fall, leaving him all the more exposed. On April 30, he announced the resignations of Ehrlichman and Haldeman — calling them "the finest public servants I have ever known." (He had been told by Henry Petersen, the head of the

Justice Department's Criminal Division, that the two men were to be named unindicted co-conspirators in the Watergate break-in.) At the same time he also fired Dean, and Richard Kleindienst, Mitchell's replacement as attorney general, resigned. Colson had been pushed out of the White House before the Watergate scandal became public. Mitchell was indicted in May 1973, along with some key Nixon fund-raisers.

When Nixon announced the resignation of Haldeman and Ehrlichman, he said that he would appoint Elliot Richardson as his new attorney general. Richardson, then serving as secretary of defense (he had replaced Melvin Laird in 1973) and formerly his secretary of health, education, and welfare, was the kind of Boston Brahmin Nixon both envied and despised, but Nixon believed that Richardson's reputation for integrity would help his image — and also that he could be trusted. But that wasn't enough to satisfy Congress, and both Houses passed a resolution calling for a prosecutor independent of the executive branch. With Richardson hedging on the guarantees of independence, the Senate Judiciary Committee made his confirmation contingent on his appointing an outside counsel with concrete guarantees. After several people turned the job down, on May 14, 1973, Richardson appointed Archibald Cox, a Harvard Law School professor and former solicitor general in Robert Kennedy's Justice Department, a man of Yankee stock and with an earned reputation for rectitude. Cox assembled a large group of highly experienced prosecutors and investigators, and set up offices in downtown Washington.[27] There was no precedent in American history for a federal criminal investigation conducted independent of the executive branch.[28] Gradually, Cox took over the Watergate case from the U.S. Attorney's office. He divided his team into separate task forces to look into the Watergate matter and the cover-up, the role of the plumbers in general, the Ellsberg break-in, the acceptance of and failure to report illegal funds, ITT's dealings with the administration, and Segretti's activities. Nixon was very worried about the Cox investigation and the White House put out the word that what had become known as "Cox's army" was made up of "left-wing Democratic zealots."

As the Cox investigators proceeded, the already beleaguered Nixon now faced another front. On May 17, 1973, the newly established Senate Select Committee on

Presidential Campaign Activities commenced public hearings into the Watergate affair. The chairman was North Carolina Democratic senator Sam Ervin, often and accurately described as folksy — a trait he drew on amply, and helpfully, in his new role of heading an inquiry into questionable activities on the part of the White House. Ervin also had often been hailed as a "great constitutional lawyer," but this was in part a relative term, as he had shown more interest in the Constitution than other senators, in part a result of his frequent citation of the law books when he had given long speeches in opposition to civil rights legislation.[29] But underneath the folksiness was a shrewd if uncluttered mind that got the point. And his constitutional conservatism also led him to be highly protective of civil liberties. Ervin became a compelling television figure, as he quoted Shakespeare and the Bible, and was now a Washington lion. For some time, most of the Republicans on the committee defended Nixon. Howard Baker, of Tennessee, the vice chairman of the committee, kept a back channel to the White House. Tapes later revealed Charles Colson telling the president, "Howard really wants to [be] with us totally," but that Baker also felt he had to maintain his "credibility" with Ervin in order to be able to negotiate with him.[30] Nixon already had his own strategy for countering the Ervin hearings. In his diary, Haldeman wrote on February 9, 1973, "He thinks we should play a hard game on this whole thing regarding the Ervin investigation." According to Haldeman, Nixon wanted to get the word spread that "foreign or communist money came in" for the antiwar demonstrations of 1972, and to tie the demonstrations to McGovern and Ted Kennedy.[31]

The nationally televised Ervin committee's hearings paraded before an astonished nation the collection of thugs, oddballs, and even smoothies who had been involved in what could now no longer be seen as the "Watergate caper" that the White House and its allies had suggested it was. Though the disclosures in the course of the hearings would have almost definitely been tracked down by Cox's team of investigators, it was important that the country *see* them being made, was witness to them, and saw for themselves the various characters involved. Though sometimes flawed and fumbling and marked by showboating, the hearings were highly revelatory — and riveting. The story unfolded like a Russian novel, full of names that were hard to keep track of, but increasingly amazing as time went on.[32] The most unusual and, if unintentionally, comic witness was Tony Ulasewicz, the private investigator hired by the White House in 1969 who had been a courier for Kalmbach, delivering the hush money to the Watergate burglars. Ulasewicz spoke proudly of placing cash-filled envelopes and keys in phone booths and lurking around corners. During his testimony, Howard Baker asked the bizarre witness, "Who thought you up?"

The testimony that caused the greatest stir, and did the most to implicate Nixon in the Watergate cover-up, came from John Dean, who was now cooperating with the prosecutors and trying to cleanse his reputation. Starting on June 25, and for the rest of the week, Dean provided electrifying testimony about the White House role, including his own as well as the president's, in perpetrating both the break-in and the cover-up. It was then that the public learned of Dean's telling Nixon there was a "cancer growing on the presidency," and about the June 21 conversation between Dean and Nixon about getting hush money for the Watergate burglars. Howard Baker's famous question, considered penetrating at the time — "What did the President know and when did he know it?" — was actually intended to undermine Dean's testimony, to try to show that Nixon's involvement was peripheral and that Dean's testimony was based on hearsay.

Among the revelations before the committee was the shredding of incriminating documents at CREEP, but the most consequential one came in July, when Alexander Butterfield, a former deputy assistant to the president, like other witnesses, was interviewed by the committee's staff before he appeared in the public hearings; as in other cases, he was matter-of-factly asked whether he thought that Nixon had taped his conversations. (Dean had said that he thought his conversations with Nixon had been taped, but not much notice was taken.) Butterfield replied that there was in fact such a taping system. When Fred Thompson, the committee's minority counsel, asked Butterfield the same question in the open hearings on July 13, his positive response set off an uproar and gave new impetus to the investigation. Though previous presidents had taped Oval Office conversations, Nixon's taping system was more thorough.

Perhaps the most disturbing event in the hearings occurred when, also on July 13, Georgia Democratic senator Herman Talmadge, a true conservative, asked Ehrlichman, during his testimony about the raid on Daniel Ellsberg's psychiatrist's office, whether he remembered the English principle that "no matter how humble a man's cottage is, even the King cannot enter without permission." Ehrlichman, who was already turning in a hostile performance, replied icily, "I am afraid that that has been considerably eroded over the years." Ehrlichman also told the committee something the significance of which wasn't perceived at the time: that Nixon had tried to involve the CIA in the cover-up. Ehrlichman testified that Nixon had said, "A man makes a grave mistake in covering up for subordinates. That was Harry Truman's error in the Hiss case, when he instructed the FBI not to cooperate." This was one of more glimpses that were to come that somewhere in there Nixon had an awareness that he was pursuing a dangerous course. While Ehrlichman played the heavy in the hearings, Haldeman was seemingly far more accommodating. But both sought to detach Nixon from the Watergate break-in and to pin the blame on Dean. Ehrlichman denied that Nixon had discussed clemency for the Watergate burglars.

The Ervin committee was highly instrumental in making it clear to the country that something was terribly wrong in the Nixon White House. Now it was for others to wrap all of the unfolding information into a legal case, and for the House of Representatives to decide what to do about all of this information — whether Nixon should be impeached. But first there would be other developments leading to, and forcing, that decision.

Once the existence of the tapes was revealed in the Ervin hearings, both the full Senate and Cox subpoenaed them. The committee Republicans couldn't defend Nixon in this matter. There has long been puzzlement as to why Nixon didn't destroy the tapes, which were the most incriminating evidence against him. Leonard Garment, Nixon's former law partner and then a special consultant to the president, advised him that destroying the tapes would be an obstruction of justice. Nixon claimed that turning over the tapes would destroy executive privilege, and he may have thought he was protecting the presidency, but at that point he was thinking about other things than the fate of future presidents. It has been speculated that Nixon wanted to keep the records to himself so that he could write from them after he was president, and that may well have been the case ("they're for later," Nixon told Haldeman), but Nixon also told his daughter Tricia that if the tapes were made public he might be impeached.[33] Nixon's refusal to destroy the tapes sealed his fate.

The man who could make mostly cool-headed, long-sighted decisions about foreign policy was now often distraught and distracted, making shortsighted and self-destructive decisions. Beginning in July 1973, Nixon made various efforts to rein in Cox's investigation, sending messages through Chief of Staff Alexander Haig or Elliot Richardson, who dutifully passed them on; Cox, of course, resisted. (In one message, Nixon sent word to Cox to "stay the hell away" from the milk fund issue.)[34] In late July, Richardson was quoted as saying that he didn't think Cox was entitled to access to the tapes.[35] When Nixon turned down both Cox's and the Senate's subpoenas of the tapes, Judge Sirica rejected the Ervin committee's request but demanded that Nixon produce the tapes so that he could examine them. On October 12 a federal court of appeals ruled that Nixon should surrender the tapes. Nixon thereupon also made the odd proposal that he would make *summaries* of the tapes available to the courts and the Ervin committee and that Senator John Stennis, a conservative Democrat from Mississippi, would verify their authenticity. Stennis, whom Nixon referred to as Judge Stennis (he was a former state judge), was what one Senate aide called a "King's Party man," one who pays obeisance to the nation's leader as such; he had spoken in praise of Nixon even as the Watergate story was breaking. (Stennis, seventy-three, was also ailing and had impaired hearing.)[36] Strangely, Ervin and Baker, for whatever reason — perhaps because the committee's investigation was petering out — agreed to the president's suggestion.[37]

Amid the Watergate scandal, another precedent was set: a vice president was forced to resign. In the summer of 1973 the *Wall Street Journal* disclosed that Vice President Spiro Agnew was under investigation by a Maryland grand jury for having taken bribes and kickbacks — over one hundred thousand dollars — from Maryland contractors for public works contracts when he was governor and that the payments had continued during his vice presidency. The image was stunning: a sitting vice president receiving envelopes stuffed with cash in his office in the Executive Office Building. At first, Agnew denounced the investigations as "damn lies"; he told his staff that Richardson, who he suspected of having presidential ambitions for 1976, was out to get him, and he even hinted that Richardson wanted a successor to Nixon who shared Nixon's pro-Israel views. Nixon was already estranged from Agnew, but recognized that in lashing out at the press Agnew had developed his own constituency. Nixon also took into account the limited value Agnew now had as insurance against his own impeachment. Told by Richardson that the case against his vice president was clear-cut, the president gave Agnew only lukewarm public support; Nixon's White House aides were convinced that Agnew had to go lest he further besmirch the president. And so on October 10 Agnew pleaded nolo contendere to the charges against him and submitted his resignation. He received a suspended sentence of three years in prison and a ten-thousand-dollar fine.

In choosing House minority leader Gerald Ford to be Agnew's successor two days later, Nixon selected a popular House member, a steady, courteous, and somewhat limited spear carrier for the White House. Ford was popular with his colleagues, and

Nixon thought he might help him in the House. (John Connally had apparently been Nixon's first choice, but House Speaker Carl Albert and Melvin Laird, now a White House adviser, told Nixon that Connally, a former Democrat and Lyndon Johnson pal, couldn't be confirmed.)[38] On the night of October 12, there was an odd spectacle in the East Room of the White House. With the cabinet, members of Congress, and the Joint Chiefs of Staff present, Nixon announced his selection of Ford, who received enthusiastic applause. A beaming Nixon, looking on, basked in Ford's reflected glory. In early December, in an improvised ceremony in the House chamber, Ford was sworn in as vice president.

Now that the matter of selecting a new vice president was settled, Nixon told Richardson, "We can go ahead and fire Cox." On Monday, October 15, Richardson warned Cox that he had until that Friday to agree to the "Stennis solution" and also to promise that he wouldn't seek further tapes or documents or there would be "serious consequences." The White House knew, of course, that Cox couldn't comply, and on Friday a White House attorney made it clear to Cox that he was facing an ultimatum; any objections to the Stennis plan were "unacceptable."[39]

The next morning, Saturday, October 20, Cox held a press conference. (Earlier that morning, Richardson had called Cox and assured him that he wouldn't carry out any order to fire him, so Cox now knew that if he went down, Richardson would go with him.)[40] The casual, crew-cut, folksy, Jimmy Stewart–like figure people saw on their television screens was quite different from the starchy, distant Harvard Law professor who had scared his students. The new manner was disarming — and devastating. Cox knew how to get the issue across in a way that people could understand. Fiddling with his jacket pocket, Cox said he was worried that "I'm getting too big for my britches." Then he got to the point, saying that the question was "whether we shall continue to be a government of laws and not of men." Cox said that he wouldn't resign and pointed out that only Richardson could fire him — thus raising the ante for Nixon. After a long day of tension and speculation, in the early evening the news bulletins began to roll in. The president had ordered Richardson to fire Cox, and Richardson had refused and resigned; his deputy, William Ruckelshaus, also refused to fire Cox and was fired; the solicitor general, Robert Bork, at the time little known (he would be nominated and rejected as a Supreme Court justice in 1987), fired Cox and was now the acting attorney general. Word also came that the FBI, now under the new director Clarence Kelley, had sealed off the offices of Cox, Richardson, and Ruckelshaus.

The nation was shaken.

The speed of the events became part of their substance, and to many, Washington suddenly felt like a banana republic. The White House had underestimated the uproar that these events would cause.[41] A few days after the Saturday Night Massacre, as it came to be called, Nixon sent word to Sirica that he would release the tapes — though some material would be omitted on the grounds of "national security" — but he would also appeal the court's ruling that he should do so.

Nixon was forced by public opinion to agree to appoint a new independent prosecutor. He chose the prominent Texas attorney Leon Jaworski as the new prosecutor, and named Ohio Republican senator William Saxbe, not one of the Senate's brightest stars, as attorney general.

As soon as Nixon had beheaded those who had defied him on the tapes, the subject of impeachment — theretofore only whispered about — became a heated public topic. Members of Congress of both parties were now issuing calls that Nixon be removed from office. There was a sudden run on the bookstores for Raoul Berger's book *Impeachment: The Constitutional Problems.* And on October 22, two days after that frightening Saturday night, House Speaker Carl Albert let it be known that he and other Democratic House leaders would ask the House Judiciary Committee to take up the question of impeachment.[42] Nixon was becoming frantic. And by then another subject that had only been whispered about, that a lot of people were uneasy about, and which according to unwritten rules the press hadn't written about — though it was a factor in what was motivating many people in power — was the question of whether Nixon was cracking up, the fears about what he might do next. The question was given legitimacy when on October 24, AFL-CIO president George Meany referred to the "dangerous emotional instability" of the president. A figure such as Meany could be quoted in the press, and so now the subject was an open one.[43] In a press conference on the night of October 26, Nixon lashed out at the press in the most open display of emotion since his "last press conference" after he lost the race for California governor in 1962. He accused television news of committing the most "outrageous, vicious, distorted reporting" he had ever experienced; and in phrases reminiscent of the self-absorbed and self-pitying passages in *Six Crises*, he also said, obviously perspiring, "The tougher it gets, the cooler I get."

By late October, the issue of the tapes was now the focus of the rising impeachment talk. A top Senate aide noted that they provided "a high-minded reason for impeachment," and it was "more clear-cut for members of Congress than corruption, break-ins or the Fourth Amendment."[44] New developments kept making things worse for Nixon. In late October, it came out that two key tapes were "missing" — setting off another bombshell — though apparently they hadn't been recorded. One was a conversation between Nixon and Mitchell, the other with Dean. (Dean had testified to the Ervin committee that Nixon "got up out of his Executive Office Building chair, went to a corner and in a barely audible voice said that he was probably foolish to have discussed Hunt's clemency with Colson.")[45] A couple of weeks later came the explosive announcement that one of the seven tapes was "inaudible" for eighteen and a half minutes. Alexander Haig announced that this was the work of "sinister forces," but it was learned later in court that Nixon had listened to the tapes at Camp David and Key Biscayne; the president's personal secretary Rose Mary Woods testified that she herself had caused the erasure by a contortion on her part, by which she inadvertently stepped on a foot pedal while answering the phone on the other side of her desk. (This became known as the "Rose Mary Stretch.") She also testified, damningly, that at Camp David the president "listened to different parts of the tapes, pushing the buttons back and forth."[46] Haldeman said later that Nixon himself had done this erasing.[47]

By mid-November, Nixon was under assault for questionable financial dealings. His tax records were being audited by the IRS. It was found that he and his attorneys had falsified records about his donation of his vice-presidential papers to the National Archives in 1969, and his tax payments had fallen off sharply after he became president. During the crisis over his tax returns, Nixon promised to give San Clemente to the nation.[48] At the same time, Nixon's net worth was reported as having more than tripled during his presidency. Responding to a question at a convention of newspaper editors at Disney World on November 17, the president of the United States looked straight into the television cameras and said, "I am not a crook."

On November 26, 1973, Nixon turned over seven tapes to Sirica but refused to release any more of them. Prosecutors who heard the tapes were convinced that Nixon was guilty of involvement in the Watergate cover-up.[49] Nixon was by now in a poor emotional state. He was paying only fitful attention to national and international affairs. According to the historian Stanley Kutler, despite Nixon's apparent resilience, former administration aides described him as tired and distracted during this period; in some meetings, he rambled and digressed even more than usual.[50] Nixon's notes for December 23, 1973, began with, "Last Christmas here?"[51]

As the new year began, Nixon felt that he was engaged in the "campaign of my life." He apparently considered resignation but said later that he felt such a move would establish a dangerous precedent; more seriously for him, it would amount to an admission of guilt.[52] In his State of the Union address in January 1974, he asserted, "It's now time for these investigations to be brought to an end, one year of Watergate is enough." (Just as he had said the year before, "Let others wallow in Watergate.") But Nixon's serial declarations that an end should be put to the Watergate business failed to put an end to it. Events were now out of his control.

On March 1, 1974, a grand jury handed down a fifty-page indictment naming Ehrlichman, Haldeman, Mitchell, and Colson, among others, for conspiracy in the cover-up. Though the indictment had been expected, as with other Watergate developments it had a greater impact than anticipated.[53] Earlier that year, Herbert Kalmbach, the president's attorney (and money conduit), pleaded guilty to charges of illegal fund-raising and was now cooperating with the prosecutors. Donald Segretti had already been convicted of committing federal crimes and gone to jail.[54] The grand jury also considered indicting Nixon, but accepted Special Prosecutor Leon Jaworski's argument that the Constitution precluded the indictment of a sitting president.[55] But Jaworski turned out to be more serious about his role than Nixon had expected. In early May, Jaworski told Haig that Nixon had been named an unindicted co-conspirator by the grand jury. In the end, the baleful record of the Nixon presidency was that twenty-five of his aides and associates were sent to jail. Another precedent was set.

Now it was up to the House Judiciary Committee to sort through the constitutional issues that had been raised by the previous events and to decide whether Nixon should be impeached. In all of American history, this question had never been seriously considered before. Despite all the calls for removing Nixon from office, for many politicians the act of actually doing so presented a hard, even agonizing question: in those times, the presidency was still a highly revered office, no matter what people thought of the occupant. The presidency stood as the tribal symbol of the nation. Actually removing a president from office was an awesome and almost frightening thing to do.

The most remarkable thing about the House Judiciary Committee's proceedings was that a group of mostly ordinary people acted extraordinarily. They rose to the task before them and some of them became giants — it seemed at times akin to the Founding Fathers — though in most cases and under other circumstances they were actually not even close to that stature. The chairman, Peter Rodino, a Democratic congressman from Newark, a pink-cheeked, silver-haired man, had not been considered an exceptional congressman, but he had a firm sense of the Constitution and the good judgment (and good advice) not to approach the matter in a highly partisan manner. He understood that if articles of impeachment were approved only by the Democratic members of the committee, much of the country would feel that the committee hadn't acted with fairness. He also evinced no zeal for his role. Other members as well were to become national figures — some of them became heroes. Barbara Jordan, a large black congresswoman from Houston, was noted for her elegant oratory; Paul Sarbanes, of Maryland, for his fine mind and thoughtfulness. James Mann, a Democrat from South Carolina, came off as the very model of a distinguished statesman but was in fact a hard-drinking and almost stereotypical junketing congressman. Counterbalancing the band of highly partisan liberals on the Democratic side was a large number of staunchly conservative Republicans. But in addition to the strong Nixon supporters, who included the vice chairman, Edward Hutchinson of

Michigan, and Charles Wiggins of California, there were four Republicans who were more to the center and undecided about Nixon's complicity: William Cohen of Maine, Tom Railsback of Illinois, Caldwell Butler of Virginia, and Hamilton Fish of New York. They were part of the "swing group," along with three southern Democrats — Mann, Walter Flowers of Alabama, and Ray Thornton of Arkansas — whose position would determine the outcome in the committee.

Rodino selected as counsel for the inquiry John Doar, who had served in the Justice Department under President Eisenhower and then became a civil rights hero in Robert Kennedy's era as attorney general. This was a crucial choice: Doar would not be seen as a partisan figure. Rodino and Doar's strategy, formed with the help of Francis O'Brien, Rodino's young administrative assistant, was to work methodically and through the swing group, so that whatever came out of the committee would be seen as having come from the center, and as having been arrived at fairly. This strategy irritated the sizable group of committee liberals who wanted to get on with impeaching Nixon.[56]

But first the committee, working without

any real precedent, had to decide what, exactly, constituted impeachment. The Constitution, relying on the English system, stipulated that it would be for "high crimes and misdemeanors" — but what were those? The document was at least clear on the fact that the House would have "the sole power of impeachment" — that is, decide the grounds on which the president could be impeached — and that the Senate would have the "sole power to try all impeach-ments," and that the punishment would be removal from office. It was also apparent from the Founders' debate on the matter that they believed, according to Raoul Berger, the author of the definitive book on the subject, that an impeachable offense need not be a crime, and that it was, ac-cording to Alexander Hamilton, intended to reach "the violation of public trust."[57]

In March, as the Judiciary Committee was proceeding, Nixon, in what was called his "campaign for survival," traveled to Chi-cago, Houston, and Nashville, talking mainly to business groups, to shore up sup-port. On these trips, Nixon attacked the Judiciary Committee's request for the tapes, calling it a "fishing expedition." At each stop, Nixon also tried to define impeach-ment as being applicable only to crimes. He seemed calmer and more in command; as usual, his shoulders formed a curve over his head, but there were fewer gestures. Also as usual, he distorted the facts of his situation. In Nashville, the president's staff planned an elaborate welcome — little Girl Scouts and others waving miniature American flags and a high school band playing (badly) "The Tennessee Waltz" — at the airport for Nixon and his wife, who arrived in her own plane from a trip to Latin America. At the Grand Ole Opry, Nixon amazed the audience, largely composed of music-business executives, by suddenly taking a yo-yo from his pocket (the symbol of Roy Acuff, one of the Opry stars) and engaging in other strange attempts at humor. The yo-yo just hung there. At Acuff's request, Nixon bonked out on the piano "Happy Birthday" to Mrs. Nixon. Back at the microphone, Nixon suggested that the crowd join him in another song. Then, with exaggerated motions, his body bent forward, his hands pawing the air, he crept toward the piano as if he were about to attack it and played "My Wild Irish Rose." This awkward clowning was very odd. In Houston, Nixon was particularly discursive, talking about everything from the Middle East to the Boy Scouts.[58]

While Nixon was taking this trip, Judge Sirica ruled that the House Judiciary Committee should be given the tapes that the White House had turned over to him. By early April, conservative members of Congress began to back away from Nixon. Vice President Ford began to talk privately about who would be in his cabinet and told John Osborne of the *New Republic* that Nixon's tendency to ramble in meetings drove him "close to distraction."[59]

Nixon was trapped. On April 30, acting under Sirica's orders, the White House released edited versions of transcripts of the tapes. The telephone-book-size document, covering forty-six conversations, was stunning. Among other things revealed in the transcripts was Nixon congratulating Dean for being "very skillful putting your fingers in the leaks that have sprung here and sprung there." Some of the tapes had "inaudible" in various — and seemingly crucial — places. And there, in black and white, was the March 21, 1973, meeting, when Dean talked to Nixon about obtaining more hush money for the Watergate burglars, and Nixon telling Dean, "It would seem to me that would be worthwhile." And, just after Nixon discussed clemency for Hunt with Dean, he uttered the line that later became part of comic routines about him, "No, it is wrong, that's for sure." The president was covering up his own role even to aides — and most likely for the record being ground out by the tapes. Out came the profanity and the anti-Semitism, the rambling conversations and the clear impression that the White House was a den of suspicion, the court of the Borgias; no one trusted anybody else.[60] The transcripts of the tapes, even edited and with all the "(expletive deleted)"s and "(inaudible)"s and "(unintelligible)"s, and the "(Further conversation unrelated to Watergate)"s, constituted a heavy blow to the Nixon presidency. Several of Nixon's political and editorial allies defected. But Nixon had held back some tapes, including the one of June 23, 1972, in which he told Haldeman that the CIA's deputy director, Vernon Walters, should tell the FBI director to "stay the hell out of this" — the most incriminating of all. The House Judiciary Committee subpoenaed more tapes and presidential diaries; Nixon refused to comply. Meanwhile, the committee hired linguists to try to decipher the (inaudible)s and other omissions, and they found numerous examples of tinkering.[61]

Months into the House Judiciary Committee's staff investigation, Doar believed he had discerned a pattern of presidential misbehavior, and then set out to build the case carefully so that committee members could see the same pattern. For six weeks the committee members listened in secret to the evidentiary material presented by the staff. While some members (and not just the predictable ones) came to the conclusion that impeachment was warranted, others said that they still needed the "smoking gun" — in a room that was full of smoke. In early July, the majority staff, working with some of the members, came up with a draft of articles of impeachment; it was critical that they make distinctions, that what they voted would be constitutionally sound and of sufficient gravity. Some issues, such as the ITT payment, were left by the wayside as too controversial — or too alarming to members of Congress.[62] During this time, Nixon took his "journey for peace" to the Middle East — a trip clouded by PR (including the required picture of Nixon at the Pyramids) — and also made his summit trip to Moscow. Nixon later admitted that these were attempts to improve his image during Watergate, but that the stratagem hadn't worked. "Too phony," he told Monica Crowley, an admiring former Nixon

White House assistant, to whom Nixon gave a series of interviews after he left office.[63]

After holding closed hearings (so as not to imitate the Ervin hearings) with the major Watergate figures, on the evening of July 24 the House Judiciary Committee began its public deliberations. Francis O'Brien, Rodino's administrative assistant and key strategist, saw to it that they were televised, so that the public would understand the issues, and, to promote a sense of intimacy, he made sure that the cameras were not visible or cluttering the room.[64] Nixon, on a ten-day "working vacation" in San Clemente, wandered from optimism to pessimism. He wrote in his diary, "I intend to live the next week without dying the death of a thousand cuts," and he called his situation his "seventh crisis in spades."[65]

Because of the almost totemistic reverence for the presidency in those times, voting to impeach Nixon was, for all but the most liberal committee members, not an easy decision. Some of the Republicans worried about the reactions of their constituents. (Nixon still had a sizable following among Republicans.) Just before the committee opened its deliberations, the members of the "swing group" — four Republicans and three Democrats — tried to find a way short of impeachment to punish the president, but they were unable to do so. They were still wriggling, but they had passed the point of no return. Rodino and his strategists thought that they would be swayed by the weight of the evidence, but their position remained uncertain to others until they cast their votes.

On the morning of the day that the Judiciary Committee was to begin its open deliberations, the Supreme Court issued a unanimous ruling that the president had to surrender all of the tapes — that it was up to the courts, not the president, to make the law. In San Clemente, after several delays, Nixon's attorney James St. Clair announced that Nixon would "respect and accept" the Supreme Court's decision.[66] Nixon, who had been fatalistic about the decision, now hoped that there were holes in it so that he could somehow evade turning over the tape of the June 23 meeting — clear proof of his role in the cover-up. Nevertheless, he began to talk with his top aides about resigning.[67]

In their opening statements, the committee members, recognizing that they were making history, spoke with decorum and dignity — the tone set by Rodino — and in most instances they listened intently to the others, a rarity in Congress. By the end of the opening speeches, Nixon's popularity had plunged to 24 percent.

On the evening of Saturday, July 27 — another fateful Saturday night — the committee approved the first article of impeachment by a vote of 27–11. The article, drafted and redrafted until the leading members thought they'd got it right, charged that Nixon had violated the oath of office to "faithfully execute the office of the president" and to "take care that the laws be faithfully executed"; that he tried to cover up the illegal break-in; that he made false statements to the public and investigators and caused his subordinates to do likewise. As the members voted, the room was utterly still; the people there sensed the gravity of the moment. All of the "swing group" members voted for the article. Afterward there was an odd feeling of sadness, not exultation, in the room, and of exhaustion — and foreboding about what was to come. Some members, including Rodino, went into the back room and wept.

At the time of the vote, Nixon was walking on the beach, and Ziegler announced that the president was certain that the House itself would not vote to impeach him.[68] Nixon had mixed feelings: resigned to a long Senate trial but also concerned that if he were convicted by the Senate he would lose all of his government emoluments, including his pension — which meant that he should resign.

On Tuesday, July 30, the committee adopted Article II, the most important one, listing various acts through which Nixon had violated his constitutional duty to "take care that the laws be faithfully executed": his use of the IRS "in violation of the constitutional rights of citizens"; wiretapping; maintaining a secret investigative force in the White House, partially paid for by campaign contributions; the cover-up; and the misuse of government agencies to interfere with investigations. The committee was establishing that certain executive behavior would not be tolerated. This article regarding Nixon's abuse of power was adopted by a vote of 28–10. As each article was adopted, the bell tolled for Nixon. Article III, saying that the president should be impeached for having failed to cooperate with an inquiry into his own impeachment, received less enthusiasm among Republicans, as the committee had yet to challenge Nixon in court on this matter, but it was adopted anyway, by a vote of 21–17. (Some Republicans felt that they had voted enough for impeachment.) Two additional proposed articles failed: one to condemn Nixon for the attacks on Cambodia, and one for evading income taxes and receiving excessive government money for his houses.

The Senate began to prepare for an impeachment trial.[69]

Almost to the end, Nixon wavered back and forth over whether to resign, but after his top aides listened to the June 23 tape, they told him he had no choice. He spent a considerable amount of time over the next few days alone in the Lincoln Sitting Room in the White House residence. And though assistant press secretary Gerald Warren announced that Nixon wouldn't resign, he was coming to terms with doing so. On August 5, under pressure from Congress, the prosecutors, and the public, Nixon released the transcripts of three withheld tapes, which, he said in a statement, "may further damage my case," and he added that a House vote to impeach was a foregone conclusion.[70] One of them was the June 23 conversation. Here, if one was needed, was the "smoking gun" that a number of members of Congress were waiting for. By now, even some of the president's strongest supporters were telling him to resign. The tape of the

June 23 conversation also revealed Nixon's anti-Semitism. He told aides to "stay away from the arts" because, he said, "The arts, you know — they're Jews, they're left-wing." (At the same time, Nixon had sought to be portrayed as doing a great deal for the arts.) And, inevitably, he talked about *Six Crises,* saying that he had been thumbing through it and "the book reads awfully well."

By early August, Nixon could no longer govern; he had lost virtually all public support, and his mental condition was terrible. Such was the turmoil and worry in Washington that there were rumors that Nixon would stage a military coup to retain his hold on power. The president was now behaving more erratically than usual. His rages were more intense, his conversations ever more rambling and odd, that some people — on Capitol Hill as well as closer to or in the White House — became highly alarmed about what Nixon might do now that he was cornered. A very worried Edward Cox, Nixon's son-in-law, told people that he had seen the president walking the halls at night, talking to pictures of former presidents. Cox also told people that the president was sleeping little and drinking a lot. But Nixon was resisting resignation. His daughters, Julie and Tricia, deeply loyal to their father, were urging him not to resign. Reports came that Nixon was denying reality. Moreover, to quit was to break his lifelong vow never to do so. (During Nixon's final days as president, Haldeman and Ehrlichman tried to wangle pardons for themselves, but Nixon's aides turned them down.) James R. Schlesinger, the secretary of defense, became so worried that he took the extraordinary step of ordering the Joint Chiefs of Staff to take no military orders directly from the White House — that any such request must be cleared through him.[71]

The King's Party men decided that Nixon had to go. On the afternoon of August 7, Senator Barry Goldwater, Senate Minority Leader Hugh Scott, and House Minority Leader John Rhodes met with the president and explained to him the realities he was facing, which of course meant that he should resign, though they never said this outright. Following his meeting with Goldwater, Scott, and Rhodes, Nixon gathered with his family in the White House solarium and told them, "We're going back to California."[72]

That night, according to Woodward and Bernstein, a distraught Nixon summoned Kissinger to the Lincoln Sitting Room and began to sob. Kissinger tried, one last time, to boost him by citing Nixon's foreign policy achievements, but Nixon was beyond solace. Nixon asked Kissinger to kneel on a rug and pray with him. And he continued to sob; when he calmed down, he began drinking again. Throughout the night, Nixon made calls to his speechwriters about his final speech as president, to be given the next morning.[73]

On the morning of August 8, Nixon met with Vice President Ford to talk briefly about the mechanics of the handover, and at nine p.m. the nation watched in amazement as the president, at his desk in the Oval Office, a flag pin in his lapel, his face looking pale and drawn, announced his resignation. He said, euphemistically, that he could no longer struggle to hold office because "I no longer have a strong enough political base in the Congress." And then, "Therefore I shall resign the presidency effective at noon tomorrow."

That night, as usual, Nixon made some postmidnight calls, one of them to his adviser Leonard Garment expressing anxiety that he would be prosecuted in the courts, and he joked, mordantly, "Some of the best political writing in this century has been done in jail."[74] Nixon added that he was referring to Gandhi, but at the time a lot of people recalled that Hitler wrote *Mein Kampf* in jail.

The story was ending with a number of "what-ifs": if the burglars hadn't botched their second Watergate break-in; if Nixon had destroyed the tapes (or simply turned off the system during highly incriminating conversations); if Sam Ervin, Archibald Cox, and Peter Rodino had been different manner of men. Would Nixon's hatreds and the numerous actions taken to carry them out have tripped him up anyway? These are questions history cannot answer, but they indicate the uncertainty of the outcome.

The morning after he announced his resignation, Nixon gathered with his grim-looking family and his staff in the East Room. "Hail to the Chief" was played for him for the last time. As he stood before the audience, inevitably he took a jab at the press, then praised his staff, added that no one in his administration was "feathering his nest," described his (hated) father as "a great man," and said once more, "My mother was a saint." Choking back sobs, he spoke of his difficult childhood and his two brothers' dying of tuberculosis, and he read from Theodore Roosevelt's diary about the death of his wife. He added that despite TR's terrible setback he had "served his country always in the arena . . . he was a man."

And then, remarkably, he told his staff, "Always remember others may hate you but those who hate you don't win unless you hate them. And then you destroy yourself."

As Nixon and his wife and children boarded the helicopter on the back lawn to take them to Andrews Air Force Base and then to California, Nixon stood in the doorway of the helicopter and gave his iconic gesture of shooting his arms in the air, his fingers forming Vs.

And then he was gone.

7
THE WIZARD

Or so it was thought.

As had occurred several times before in his career, the assumption that Richard Nixon was truly gone from public life was a vast underappreciation of the man's extraordinary resilience, his deeply embedded determination to rise again. In a large sense, that was how he defined his own life. He had come back from the Checkers fund scandal, his narrow defeat by John F. Kennedy, and his loss of the California governorship. He was obsessed with overcoming crises. Perhaps people should have paid more attention to Nixon's parting comments about Theodore Roosevelt — or TR, as he was called — who, it seemed, he now set out to emulate, even referring to himself as RN. Nixon admired Roosevelt as an indomitable man of action, a man who never gave up. Nixon's new battle wasn't for elective office but perhaps something even more important to him: respectability. Though now a broken man, he methodically plotted his comeback, as he had done before in his political career with remarkable success. He was determined once again to overcome his opponents. To fix his place in history. To be respected as an elder statesman. To shed the appellation "Tricky Dick." Under the code name "The Wizard" — of course his effort had to have a code name — Nixon set out to establish himself as an elder statesman, a political and foreign policy sage.

After he returned to San Clemente in August 1974, Nixon called friends, sometimes crying, saying that he simply couldn't take any more. The special prosecutor was still at work and calls were rising for Nixon to be prosecuted. He told former aides that the media wouldn't let up on him. "They won't be satisfied," he said, "until they have me in jail."[1] Yet Nixon also worried that if he were to accept a pardon, he would be admitting guilt — until his attorney pointed out that, given all the publicity, it was impossible that he could get a fair trial.[2]

The new president, Gerald Ford, was under considerable pressure to decide whether to pardon Nixon. Ford faced a number of competing arguments. A widely held view was that Nixon should not be above the law; even the American Bar Association took this position. Against that were some practical as well as even humane considerations. Nixon had already paid a grievous price for his actions, and some members of Congress, including Republicans who had thought Nixon should go, believed that, in the words of Senate Republican leader Hugh Scott, "enough is enough." There was considerable concern that Nixon wouldn't physically survive a legal process that could take years. Nixon's son-in-law David Eisenhower, as well as other members of Nixon's family, lobbied Ford to pardon the ex-president. Leon Jaworski, the special prosecutor, along with his top staff members, was concerned about the years that a prosecution of Nixon would take and worried about the problem of Nixon's ever receiving a fair trial, given all the publicity about his misdeeds. By forwarding to the White House a memo by a staff member, Jaworski signaled that he would not oppose a pardon.[3] Ford also took care to be certain that a pardon was within his constitutional power, and he relied heavily on a Supreme Court decision that accepting a pardon was an admission of guilt.

Ford was anxious to get the question behind him and to get on with governing. He had tried to calm the nation by saying when he was sworn in as president, "Our long national nightmare is over." Though Ford was still angry with Nixon for having lied to him while he was vice president, and though he "had lost almost all respect for his former friend" (according to Nixon's biographer Melvin Small), Ford took into account Nixon's frail condition and decided by the end of August that he should be pardoned.[4] After exacting from a most reluctant Nixon a mild statement of contrition, Ford announced on September 8 that he would pardon him, saying that Nixon and his family had "suffered enough."

Though it became increasingly clear that Ford had acted wisely, there was a huge outcry against the pardon; Ford's popularity ratings plummeted. Amid the furor, Ford took the unusual step of offering to appear before the House Judiciary Committee to explain why he had given Nixon the pardon — the first time since George Washington that a president had appeared before Congress — and testified truthfully that there had been no quid pro quo between himself and Nixon. (Some have written that Nixon called Ford and offered to give back the pardon but, given the stakes and Nixon's condition, one has to wonder if the offer, if made, was heartfelt.)

Following the pardon, Nixon, upset by the adverse public reaction, was in bad shape emotionally and physically. Besides the ignominious end of his presidency, he was suffering from a serious recurrence of phlebitis (an inflammation of the leg that can cause blood clots), from which he had suffered off and on for years, that had flared up badly during his last presidential trip to the Middle East. (In Egypt, though in great pain and limping, he insisted — TR-like — on hiking around the pyramids.) His White House doctor flew out to California and told the press that Nixon was "a ravaged man who has lost the will to fight," and that he was suffering from "severe physical strain and physical fatigue."[5] This set off speculation about the state of Nixon's mental condition, which in fact wasn't good. (A more serious recurrence of phlebitis a couple of months later nearly took his life.)

At the same time that Nixon was in such poor condition — he had lost the office he had sought for so long, had been humiliated and essentially run out of town — he also showed himself to be capable of remarkable self-knowledge, and of being philosophical about his fate. Talking with one of his aides in San Clemente in October 1974, he ruminated about what had led him to this place. "What starts the process," Nixon said, "are the laughs and snubs and slights that you get when you are a kid." Nixon continued, "But if you are reasonably intelligent and if your anger is deep enough and strong enough, you learn that you can change those attitudes by excellence, personal gut performance, and those who had everything are sitting on their fat butts." He had appointed tough guys as his aides, he said, because he wanted people who were like him, fighters. Referring to his going out for high school and college football, he said that the fact that he wasn't a good athlete "was the very reason I tried and tried and tried. To get discipline for myself and to show others that here was a guy who could dish it out and take it. Mostly I took it." He said that by working very hard "you get out of the alley and on your way. In your own mind, you have nothing to lose, so you take plenty of chances. . . . It's a piece of cake until you get to the top. You find that you can't stop playing the game because it is part of you. . . . So you are lean and mean and resourceful and you continue to walk on the edge of the precipices because over the years you have become fascinated by how close to the edge you can walk without losing your balance." When the aide commented that this time, at the end, there had been a difference, Nixon replied softly, "Yes. This time we had something to lose."[6]

From the time he left office, Nixon was deeply engaged in an attempt to control his own history. A matter of great importance was to keep unflattering information from becoming public. He tried to retain control of his presidential papers, despite an agreement he had signed earlier to turn them over to the National Archives. In fact, Bill Gully, a longtime White House military aide, began shipping papers to San Clemente at the same time that Nixon was saying farewell to his staff. Gully also brought several boxes with him to Nixon's new West Coast headquarters on the weekend after Nixon resigned and advised Nixon's aides that all the papers should be shipped out before Ford's staff, still settling in, realized what was happening. Back in Washington, Gully continued to prepare boxes for shipment — in all there were enough documents to fill three railroad boxcars — but was caught shortly thereafter when by chance a

Ford aide discovered truckloads of them in the White House driveway on a Saturday night, and the shipments were interrupted. A significant number of his documents were destroyed not long after Nixon left office, by use of a White House chemical shredder.[7] (After a revelation in the *Washington Post,* also stopped was a shipment of crates holding two million dollars' worth of gifts, including elaborate pieces of jewelry, that had been given to members of the Nixon family by foreign leaders. Under the law, foreign gifts worth over fifty dollars are to be turned over to the federal government.)[8] An act of Congress in 1974 held that all of Nixon's presidential papers and tapes belonged to the federal government and were to be stored in the National Archives and released to the public "at the earliest reasonable date." The law also said that the Archives would have sole control over the Nixon material. Through extensive maneuvering, Nixon was able to ward off the Archives' release of numerous papers about Watergate and Vietnam, among other things, giving him ample time to work at rehabilitating his reputation. Much of "operation Wizard" took place against the backdrop of Ronald Reagan's presidency, marked by bombast against the Soviet Union, contempt for détente, and attempts to cut deeply or eliminate domestic programs — all producing among many people a nostalgia for Nixon's more moderate policies.

Determined to write his own history — and also needing money (though he did receive a federal pension) after paying hundreds of thousands of dollars in back taxes — only weeks after he left the White House, Nixon set out to write a memoir, for which he received a $2.5 million advance. His book *RN: The Memoirs of Richard Nixon* (Nixon had insisted on beginning with the initials) was largely based on his personal diaries and presented his own view of events. He was aided in this and later literary efforts by the ample staff the federal government provided for his exile. When *RN* was published in 1978, it sold a remarkable 330,000 copies in the first six months.[9] But his battle to redefine himself also received setbacks from events he could not control. At the end of 1974 and into 1975, Ehrlichman, Haldeman, Colson, Mitchell, Dean, Kalmbach, Liddy, McCord, and some lesser former White House aides were sentenced to prison terms.

In 1977, as he was still preparing his book, Nixon took another major step to advance himself politically and financially by granting a series of interviews to David Frost, the famed British broadcaster, for a fee of six hundred thousand dollars plus 20 percent of the profits. After intensive negotiations over the television deal, in March of that year Nixon sat down with Frost for twenty-eight and three-quarter hours. Frost was a skilled interviewer, but Nixon, the practiced debater, was a difficult interviewee. And he was awkward in between the sessions; one day, as Nixon and Frost were walking back to the studio, Nixon suddenly asked a startled Frost, who was in California with a girlfriend, "Did you do any fornicating this weekend?"[10] When the series was broadcast in May, it won a huge worldwide audience, with forty-five million viewers in America alone. In the interviews, Nixon displayed his wide-ranging knowledge of foreign policy, talking of leaders he had known, but what got the most attention were Nixon's comments about Watergate. In reply to Frost's questions, Nixon sometimes displayed his curious mixture of contrition, self-pity, and aggressiveness, saying he had "let down" his friends and the American citizens, and he admitted that "I did abuse the power I had as president." He denied that he had been involved in the payments to silence the Watergate burglars, but admitted, "I said things that were not true." He said that by the time he resigned "I was crippled." Again showing self-knowledge, Nixon said, "I brought myself down. I gave them a sword, and they stuck it in. And they twisted it with relish. And, I guess, if I'd been in their position, I'd have done the same thing." When Frost asked Nixon about the Huston plan, Nixon replied aggressively, revealing his exceptional view of presidential authority: "When the president does it that means it is not illegal."[11]

Frost later recalled, "Socially, President Nixon was polite and affable, but always with that Nixonian reserve, the sense that there was a permanent invisible shield he had erected between himself and other people. There was just one rare occasion — one *very rare* occasion — when for twenty minutes the shield lifted and a carefree Richard Nixon emerged. The tapings were over and the first four shows had been edited — only two of which had aired — but we were leaving California and I felt I should take my leave of him after such a demanding month. To my surprise, he greeted me with 'Hello David' — the first time he had used my first name in the entire time."[12]

And then, as Frost wrote in his book *I*

Gave Them a Sword, Nixon did more unusual things. He graciously offered to show Frost and his girlfriend his San Clemente home (the tapings had taken place in a studio up the road). Then he took Frost's girlfriend by the arm — a rare gesture on his part, given his uneasiness with women — and, pointing toward a window, said, "Out there is China"; next he pointed to a certain room and said, "Brezhnev slept in that room." He continued, "A great swordsman. The Russians are, you know." He asked them if they'd read *Anna Karenina.* "Very romantic," Nixon commented, then ordered up a fine white wine and instructed Manolo Sanchez, still his valet, "Get the caviar the Shah sent us for Christmas, Manolo."

Frost wrote that as he drove away, he thought of Nixon as a man with "a good mind, with a thirst for nobility. A sad man, who so wanted to be great."[13]

The interviews made for compelling television. Nixon's approval ratings rose strongly.

Above all, Nixon wanted to be seen as an elder statesman, the high priest of foreign policy, and he set out to speak, travel, and write to establish his expertise. This was also, of course, an effort to deflect attention from the more unfortunate aspects of his presidency. He spoke often about how his overture to China had caused the Soviet Union to seek better relations with the United States. In early 1976 he accepted an invitation to visit China, the scene of his greatest triumph, infuriating President Ford and other Republicans. (Nixon had kept in touch with both Mao Zedong and Zhou Enlai, both sides agreeing that U.S.–China relations needed to be deepened.) Ford, running for the Republican nomination against a strong challenge by Ronald Reagan, managed to get in a visit of his own to China before Nixon's return trip, but Ford's didn't go particularly well. Nixon's arrival in China in February 1976 was subdued, compared to his presidential welcome four years earlier, but the Chinese laid on a busy schedule, which included a talk with the frail Mao — who during Nixon's bout with phlebitis had called him "one of the greatest statesmen in history." At dinners, Nixon responded to toasts with his own policy statements — on relations between the two nations, on criticism of the Shanghai Communiqué — that suggested he was still, or thought he was still, president: "There is much work to be done. But we are determined to complete it."[14] (During the trip, still straining to be one of the guys, he made some bizarre comments to reporters about geishas: "You sit down and play games.") Following this trip, Kissinger called Nixon and said that Ford would like to send an emissary to him to be briefed on the China trip; Nixon insisted that he would speak only to Brent Scowcroft, Ford's national security adviser. Nixon won.

In several ways, Nixon was playing a fantasy presidency. In the summer of 1978, he planned to make a six-week world tour, meeting a dozen heads of state — but some let it be known that they had no wish to see him, and press commentary in several countries about his possible visit was negative. Henry Kissinger and William Rogers advised him that his timing was all wrong, that it was too soon, and so, in late August, after signing a contract for another book, Nixon announced that the trip had been "postponed" so that he could work on the book.[15] Soon thereafter, he did accept an invitation to speak at the Oxford Union, the historic debating society at one of Britain's greatest universities, and in late November 1978 set off for it, stopping in Paris, where he made a successful appearance on a popular television program. His visit to

Britain was more problematic. It had been widely denounced and he was greeted by protesters. But Nixon seemed to enjoy the protesters (he'd been through that before), and in his talk he told his audience, "I'm not going to just fade away and live the good life in San Clemente." He spoke of his determination to continue to engage in world issues, and handled questions with dexterity; at the end he received an ovation. He was on his way. Upon his return to the United States, he told a reporter, "A man is not finished when he is defeated," adding, "He is finished when he quits."[16]

By the late 1970s, Nixon had become bored with the confines of life in California, feeling isolated and that he was living in a house that was too small for the kind of entertaining that he needed to do to fulfill his rehabilitation plans, so he and Pat moved to New York in 1980 to be, as he put it, on the "fast track."[17] New York would be a more suitable place for cultivating the foreign policy establishment and important media and business figures. (In keeping with a pattern, Nixon set off something of an uproar by selling his California home, which he had promised to give to the government, to some wealthy California businessmen, making a tidy profit.) And then this far from gregarious man began a salon in his new brownstone in New York City, systematically entertaining celebrities, businessmen, politicians, policy makers, and occasionally journalists, in mostly stag dinners (among other reasons because of the blue language used at these events), off-the-record, and often in the manner of seminars on a particular topic — finance, the economy, or even Shakespeare, many times with a visiting scholar as a featured guest. Those who had attended spoke highly of these special evenings, and Nixon's house became the place to go.

The rituals for these dinners were as methodical as was their purpose: at 7:00 p.m. sharp, Nixon somewhat awkwardly greeted his guests in the foyer; this was followed by cocktails in the upstairs library, with Nixon mixing the drinks (he specialized in dry martinis), light conversation over hors d'oeuvres served by Chinese waiters — the house was done up in Chinese decor as an unsubtle reminder of his great triumph — and then by a dinner of excellent Chinese food accompanied by fine wines (Nixon liked to discourse on wines) and a conversation, usually directed by Nixon, about the topic of the evening. Lighter conversation followed in the living room, with Nixon often telling stories. The evenings ended at exactly 10:30 p.m. At that point, Nixon was wont to look at the clock and comment, "Well I promised to get so and so to the local house of disrepute by 11:00, so I guess we'd better call it a night."[18] Nixon, who had rarely enjoyed life, did enjoy his time in New York — dining at fine restaurants, hobnobbing with celebrities, meeting visiting heads of state, attending football games, and being a celebrity himself. He wrote articles for the *New York Times* and *Foreign Affairs*. Nixon bathed in his recognition.[19] Newspapers and news magazines wrote celebratory pieces about his "comeback." This was a long way from the threat of prison or the disgraced, isolated exile in California.

As part of his effort to establish himself as an elder statesman, Nixon one way or another got himself included in other presidents' foreign policy events, and was therefore seemingly sought out by them for his advice. Though Jimmy Carter loathed Nixon, and had essentially run against him in 1976, he invited Nixon to the White House once — for a dinner with Chinese leaders in January 1979 — only at the insistence of the Chinese.[20] After Nixon took another trip to China later that year, he was ranked in a Gallup poll as one of the most ten admired men in the world.[21] In 1981, Nixon decided that he wanted to attend Anwar Sadat's funeral in Cairo (earlier in the year, he had attended the Shah's funeral, also in Cairo), and Alexander Haig, then Ronald Reagan's secretary of state, urged Reagan to include Nixon in the official delegation, along with former presidents Ford and Carter — making for a rather tense threesome at first, but putting Nixon back in the limelight.[22] (This trip led Senator Robert Dole, who had been sarcastic about Nixon before, to quip that the three men represented "Hear no evil, see no evil, and evil.") After Sadat's funeral, Nixon slipped away and, having told no one but Haig of his plans, traveled elsewhere in the Middle East — Saudi Arabia, Jordan, Tunisia, Morocco — meeting heads of state, and then to Paris, where he prepared a report to the president, a summary of which he released to the press. Upon returning to the United States, an ebullient Nixon began to lay plans for trips to China, Eastern Europe, and Africa — and perhaps another trip to Russia, where he'd mend the now-frayed détente. He spoke of great leaders he had known and read to a visitor an excerpt from a TR speech, which talked of "the man in the arena" who "does actually strive to do the deeds . . . who at the best knows the triumphs of high achievement and who at the worst, if he fails, at least fails while daring greatly."[23]

Nixon made his most devious maneuver in his efforts to be seen as an adviser to presidents by blackmailing Bill Clinton. He let it be known that if Clinton didn't show him the proper respect he would write an op-ed article in a prominent newspaper criticizing his conduct of foreign policy. After some lobbying by Nixon allies, Clinton had already phoned Nixon, but now, in March 1993, shortly after the blackmail and before a summit meeting between Clinton and Russian president Boris Yeltsin that was to take place in Vancouver, Clinton invited Nixon to meet him in the White House; though the fact of the meeting itself was made public, it was held in the evening so that no press would be around to take pictures or ask questions.[24]

Nixon published eight more books between 1980 and 1992, most of them about foreign policy. (One was titled *In the Arena,* as a further homage to Theodore Roosevelt.) The books were mostly turgid and not very revealing, and though there were interesting passages, he shaped the past as it suited him. There's no clear evidence that his writings had a substantive impact on policy, but aside from producing income, they were part of Nixon's elaborate effort to merchandise himself as a sage.

He gave lectures to rapt audiences in the United States, insisting on a single microphone with no podium, so that everyone could see that he wasn't relying on notes. He spoke in his authoritative manner — head somewhat lowered, jowls shaking slightly, his voice deep. His long disquisitions on foreign leaders he had known, and what some of them had said to him, took on an aspect of name-dropping, but they largely impressed his audiences. In 1984, at an annual convention of newspaper editors, some of whom had helped end his career, he offered his political opinions, and he presented what much of his audience saw as a virtuoso tour of the politics of each state; he predicted that Walter Mondale would pick Gary Hart or Lloyd Bentsen as his running mate, and that Reagan would win by a hair. (Mondale of course picked Geraldine Ferraro and lost forty-nine states.) In 1986, he repeated his "lion's den" performance by appearing at a convention of newspaper publishers, dazzling his audience with his *tour d'horizon* of the world.

Standing before the prestigious group, Nixon pronounced Gary Hart the front-runner for the 1988 nomination and predicted, also incorrectly as it turned out, that Hart would prevail over George H. W. Bush; he received a standing ovation at the end of his talk. (Michael Dukakis, the Democratic nominee in 1988, lost to Bush by a wide margin.) But even when he was wrong, Nixon still showed that he knew a great deal and had a capacious memory as well as the capacity to speak with apparent authority, enough to impress people who had had little regard for him in earlier times. When, following his 1986 performance before the publishers, *Newsweek* wanted to write yet another story about "Nixon's comeback," the ex-president let it be known that he would cooperate only if his picture was on the cover. And so it was.

Sometimes when he addressed groups he was dead-on. In 1984, Nixon sent word to Newt Gingrich, then a rabblerousing backbench congressman, that he wanted to meet with some of the newer Republican members of Congress. And so one morning in June, he met with about a dozen young congressmen in a large suite in Washington's Madison Hotel. An obviously awkward and uncomfortable Nixon met them in the foyer, but didn't seem to know what to do — where they should sit, whether he should talk — talk about what? An aide said, "Mr. President, let's go into the other room and sit down." They did so, but more awkwardness followed, with a formal Nixon making tentative suggestions of what they should talk about. After an awkward silence, happily for Nixon, one congressman suggested that he talk to them about foreign policy; Nixon brightened and talked with great confidence and authority about what was going on in the world — enthralling the young congressmen. He then switched to domestic politics. At the time, the received wisdom in political circles was that Republicans, running on a ticket with the popular Ronald Reagan, who was up for reelection, would gain about forty House seats. Nixon talked about the past voting histories of specific districts and even counties, and predicted a far lower number of Republican gains — fourteen, considerably fewer than anyone else thought — and that was precisely what happened.[25]

Though he was not invited to Republican conventions, Nixon made extensive efforts to be politically active behind the scenes: phone calls, memoranda to the candidate, on occasion a chat with the candidate. He tried to help Ford win the 1976 election and also to help Reagan defeat Carter in 1980. Nixon considered Carter the kind of weakling he disdained. Nixon also persistently made phone calls as a way of keeping himself informed; he would ask, for example, who was running the campaign in some obscure district and get the latest poll numbers.[26] Sometimes he was invited to Republican fund-raisers. When Nixon told Reagan campaign aides in 1980 that their man would win New York, they laughed; Reagan won New York. After Nixon hinted to Reagan aides that there might be a place for him in a Reagan presidency, one of them remarked that Nixon was "hallucinating."[27]

Following Reagan's victory, Nixon lobbied hard for his former chief of staff Alexander Haig to be made secretary of state, over Reagan's apparent first choice, George Shultz, whom Nixon referred to as a "candy ass." When Haig was chosen for the post, Nixon felt that, having supported both Reagan and his secretary of state, he was all the more the political sage, all the more needed as a counselor, and he kept up the calling and the writing of notes. (In June 1982, the bullying, tempestuous Haig, Nixon's most helpful advocate in Washington, was pushed out and replaced by Shultz.) Perhaps Nixon was living in his own hallucinatory world, but few people didn't take his calls, even if they gulped at finding the ex-president on the line.[28]

After a year and a half in New York, the restless, rootless Nixon decided in 1981 to move again, this time to a more rural and private setting in Saddle River, New Jersey. This provided him not only seclusion from the hustle and bustle — and, to him, the loose morals — of New York, but also still more living space, and, he thought, a healthier setting for his visiting grandchildren, to whom he was becoming attached. And it wasn't a long commute to his New York office. He was a frenzy of activity: traveling to Europe, taking another trip to China, giving interviews, sending papers on his foreign policy views (particularly on U.S.–Soviet policy) to opinion leaders, publishing books, attending a strange reunion of his former aides in Washington on the tenth anniversary of his reelection, where he was lionized. It was like a celebration of a successful team. *Time* published a full page of his thoughts and called him "the world's unique and ubiquitous elder statesman without portfolio" —

and other print media wrote of his "redemption."[29]

One Nixon gambit for getting attention to and respect for his foreign policy views was to write a "confidential" memorandum to policy makers and then leak it to friendly journalists. One of these maneuvers, in 1992, landed a Nixon memo on the front page of the *New York Times.* The "confidential" memo, which called George H. W. Bush's policy in response to Russia's moves toward democracy "pathetically inadequate," made a big splash — as Nixon intended.[30]

After moving to New Jersey, Nixon continued his methodical efforts to fix his place in history. In Saddle River, he hosted a series of dinner-seminars with journalists who weren't of age during Watergate. (These soirees were arranged by Roger Stone, a flashy Washington lobbyist, conservative activist, and former protégé of Charles Colson.) At these dinners, Nixon, as usual, discoursed on foreign policy and on politics, for example setting forth how Ronald Reagan should run his reelection campaign — trying to make a positive impression on the younger journalists. But on occasion the evenings didn't go as smoothly as Nixon hoped. John Fund, at the time a conservative activist (and later a *Wall Street Journal* columnist), agreed to attend a dinner on one condition — that Nixon talk about domestic policy for the first forty-five minutes — and his condition was accepted. But when during this dinner Fund raised numerous questions about Nixon's domestic policy — mainly to press him on his inconsistencies, which the conservative Fund saw as sheer opportunism — an obviously uncomfortable Nixon perspired profusely and a few times tried to change the subject.[31]

Though he seemed to some more mellow, in fundamental ways Nixon hadn't changed. He was still a schemer. He still had his seething hatreds. Privately, he still railed at the press, at the "liberal establishment," "fucking academics," "goddam Ivy Leaguers." They were all spoiled, he said; he hadn't been pampered the way they had been. He was, he said, "culturally different" — and, he was sure, they hated him.[32] But he no longer had his hands on the levers of power, so his anger and paranoia were no longer dangerous. Financially comfortable as he now was, he still resented those who had been born to privilege. He was the self-made man, the striver, and he shared TR's admiration of strivers. (This though Theodore Roosevelt himself was born to privilege.) The odd thing about Nixon's "redemption" was that it was as a result of his own efforts among the "elites," whom he had long viewed with disdain (mixed with envy), that he had risen. Polls showed that majorities of Americans still disliked him, and most even thought he should have been put on trial. And, as Nixon himself understood, some of his draw of audiences rested on sheer curiosity rather than just an eagerness to hear his views. They come to see him, he told an interviewer, "because they say, 'What makes this guy tick?' "[33] He also understood that he was taking his place in another American myth; he told another interviewer, "Renewal. Americans are crazy about renewal."[34]

For his legacy to last, and seeking the recognition he felt he deserved, Nixon continued to long for a library in his name. Previous ex-presidents had had libraries built in their honor: expensive institutions — some of them shrines — paid for by both private and public funds, to hold their papers and memorabilia. They were often the settings for conferences and, in later years, activities by the former president. But, under the circumstances, Nixon's presidential library would be different: it would be privately funded and managed, it wouldn't contain his papers (which were being held by the government), and it wouldn't be directed by the National Archives. The presidential library without presidential papers was essentially a museum, one that showcased Nixon's achievements more than his failures. A director, chosen by Nixon himself, would decide which items would be displayed and who would see them.[35] (His daughters were to carry out their father's mission. In a program aired on January 1, 2003, Julie Nixon Eisenhower told Larry King that at the suggestion of a friend of her father's the Watergate Wing of the library — the largest display — was kept dark "so that you want to move on." She added, "If you want to stand there in the dark and read the panels, you can. But you really kind of want to move yourself along.")

In July 1990, the Nixon Library was opened in Yorba Linda, where he was born, and on its grounds was Nixon's modest first home. The opening of this faux-library was a grand spectacle; for the first time, four presidents and their wives appeared together: the Nixons, the George H. W. Bushes, the Fords, and the Reagans. Their presence was testimony to a sort of "Presidents Club," in which the tiny number of living ex-presidents feel a kind of bond: they alone understand the pressures and the difficulties of the office and they are protective of it. On March 11, 1992, Nixon even staged a conference at the Nixon Library on "America's Role in the Emerging World," which President Bush felt compelled to attend. (After many years of bitter wrangling over control of the library, and after lobbying by Nixon allies, Congress in 2004 passed a law making the place an official, government-paid presidential library, run by the National Archives, which would transfer the presidential papers to Yorba Linda over the years. Federal direction of the library was to commence in 2007, the Watergate Wing was to be dismantled, and various other changes in the operation of the library were to be made.[36] The National Archives would retain copies of the tapes, presumably to guard against the kind of doctoring that those tapes already at Nixon's museum had undergone. In 2000, as a result of a suit brought by Nixon in 1980, the government paid the estate $18 million for papers it had seized in 197 Though other former presidents had o their papers, in Nixon's case the ment claimed ownership. After tw of litigation a settlement was reached; Nixon had originally sued for $200 million.)[37]

On June 22, 1993, Pat Nixon, who had been in failing health, died. Nixon sobbed almost uncontrollably at her funeral; for all its strangeness, Nixon considered theirs a sturdy marriage — it had lasted fifty-three years — and a good partnership. Nixon himself died of a severe stroke less than a year later, on April 22, 1994, at the age of eighty-one.

Nixon would have been pleased with his funeral. On April 29, a large number of grandees gathered in Yorba Linda; President Clinton and his wife as well as the three living ex-presidents and their wives were in attendance. Henry Kissinger and even Bob Dole, their voices cracking, gave eulogies. Clinton tried graciously to put Nixon's public life in perspective and end the rancor, saying, "May the day of judging President Nixon on anything less than his entire life and career come to a close." (This had been an issue among Clinton's staff, and liberals across the country were furious.) The scene was that of a great man, an elder statesman, being laid to rest.

In the end, though Nixon was far from niversally popular, his "Wizard" project succeeded. He had worked his wonders to conjure yet another version of himself. It was a remarkable performance.

In his lifetime, no one was more revealing about Nixon than Nixon. He took the public into his inner chambers. This secretive man often told the public what was in his head; he talked openly about his obsessions and hatreds. He could be strikingly reflective about himself. Not only were there his remarkable comments to an aide in San Clemente on why he had ended up where he had, but also, while he was living in New York, Nixon gave a revelatory interview to Bob Greene, a *Chicago Sun-Times* columnist. Nixon spoke about his propensity for distancing himself from people. He pointed out that he was a formal man, and always worked in a coat and tie — even when alone at home. He said that, unlike other politicians, he did not like "touching the flesh," as Lyndon Johnson did; that he did not believe in letting one's hair down, even with friends, saying, "I believe you should keep your troubles to yourself." And then, perhaps offering the secret to his remarkable resilience, Nixon said, "I don't allow my feelings to get hurt," and he added, "If I had feelings I probably wouldn't have even survived."[38]

Nixon did have feelings when great tragedy struck: when his presidency lay in ruins; when his wife died. His daughters loved him, and toward the end of his life he enjoyed the company of his family — for whom he'd had little time when he was in the White House. But there was a part of Nixon that didn't get involved, hung back, particularly in human relations. He had a detachment that helped him survive. He seemed to steel himself against the past — he spoke often about the importance of not "looking back," and advised people that they shouldn't care what others thought of them. He essentially lived and died a lonely, unconnected man.

It has often been said that "but for" Watergate, Nixon would have been a good, even great, president. Some argue that his achievements in domestic policy, or foreign policy, overshadow the unfortunate denouement of his presidency. Yet aside from the lingering questions about these policies, and however large the achievements were, in this case there is no "but for." The events that caused Nixon's downfall commenced as soon as he became president, and came from within his soul. The traits that led to it — the paranoia, the anger, the determination to wreak revenge, the view that the opposition should be destroyed, even the excessive drinking — cannot be excised from the Nixon presidency. Their effects on Nixon's behavior caused a great deal of national turmoil and not a little, or unwarranted, fear that a democratically elected government was out of control, defying the limits of the democratic system. His actions were far outside the bounds of governing; they were often illegal but, beyond that, they violated constitutional restraints.

They leave the historic question of whether this otherwise smart, talented man, but most peculiar and haunted of presidents, was fit to occupy the most powerful office in the nation — and large room for doubt that he was.

NOTES

Introduction

1. David Greenberg, *Nixon's Shadow: The History of an Image* (New York: Norton, 2003), p. 235.

Chapter One: Up from Yorba Linda

1. Greenberg, *Nixon's Shadow,* p. 9.
2. Melvin Small, *The Presidency of Richard Nixon* (Lawrence, Kansas: The University of Kansas, 1999), p. 3.
3. Roger Morris, *Richard Milhous Nixon* (New York: Henry Holt and Company, 1960), p. 185.
4. Small, *The Presidency of Richard Nixon,* p. 4.
5. Morris, *Richard Milhous Nixon,* pp. 142–45.
6. Small, *The Presidency of Richard Nixon,* p. 5.

7. Morris, *Richard Milhous Nixon,* pp. 168–69.

8. Ibid., pp. 177–78.

9. Kati Marton, *Hidden Power: Presidential Marriages That Shaped Our Recent History* (New York: Pantheon, 2001), p. 173.

10. Garry Wills, *Nixon Agonistes: The Crisis of the Self-Made Man* (Boston: Houghton Mifflin, 1969), p. 172.

CHAPTER TWO: THE RISE AND FALL AND RISE OF RICHARD NIXON

1. Greenberg, *Nixon's Shadow,* p. 3.

2. Ibid., p. 22.

3. Lewis Chester, Godfrey Hodgson, and Bruce Page, *An American Melodrama: The Presidential Campaign of 1968* (New York: Viking Press, 1969), p. 244.

4. Wills, *Nixon Agonistes,* p. 77.

5. Richard Nixon, *Six Crises* (New York: Doubleday, 1962), pp. 1–71.

6. Thomas C. Reeves, *The Life and Times of Joe McCarthy* (New York: Stein and Day, 1982), p. 223.

7. Greenberg, *Nixon's Shadow,* p. 29.

8. Sam Tanenhaus, "Mud Wrestling," *New York Times Book Review,* February 1, 1998, p. 12.

9. Morris, *Richard Milhous Nixon,* pp. 657–736.

10. Small, *The Presidency of Richard Nixon,* p. 14.

11. Morris, *Richard Milhous Nixon,* p. 858.

12. Small, *The Presidency of Richard Nixon,* p. 15.

13. Morris, *Richard Milhous Nixon,* p. 818.

14. Wills, *Nixon Agonistes,* p. 114.

15. Nixon, *Six Crises,* p. 102.

16. Small, *The Presidency of Richard Nixon,* p. 16.

17. Ibid., p. 17.

18. Theodore H. White, *The Making of the President, 1960* (New York: Atheneum, 1961), p. 195.

19. Robert Dallek, *An Unfinished Life: John F. Kennedy, 1917–1963* (Boston: Little Brown, 2003), p. 294.

20. Ibid., p. 295.

21. Ibid.

22. Small, *The Presidency of Richard Nixon,* p. 21.

23. White, *The Making of the President,* p. 52.

24. Wills, *Nixon Agonistes,* p. 67.

25. Kevin Phillips, *The Emerging Republican Majority* (New Rochelle: Arlington House, 1969), p. 189.

26. Small, *The Presidency of Richard Nixon,* p. 24.
27. Phillips, *The Emerging Republican Majority,* p. 465.
28. Wills, *Nixon Agonistes,* pp. 67–69.
29. Ibid., p. 90; Elizabeth Drew, "Washington Report," *Atlantic,* January 1969.

CHAPTER THREE: GOVERNING STYLE

1. Rowland Evans Jr. and Robert D. Novak, *Nixon in the White House: The Frustration of Power* (New York: Random House, 1971), p. 10.
2. George Christian, *The President Steps Down* (New York: Macmillan, 1970), p. 245.
3. Evans and Novak, *Nixon in the White House,* p. 10.
4. Ibid., pp. 9–11.
5. Ibid., p. 51.
6. Small, *The Presidency of Richard Nixon,* p. 40.
7. Evans and Novak, *Nixon in the White House,* pp. 21–28.
8. Walter Isaacson, *Kissinger* (New York: Simon and Schuster, 1992), p. 174.
9. Small, *The Presidency of Richard Nixon,* p. 220.
10. Ibid., p. 18.

11. John Ehrlichman, *Witness to Power: The Nixon Years* (New York: Simon and Schuster, 1982), pp. 37–38.

12. Under its generic name phenytoin: *Physicians' Desk Reference,* 2006, p. 2154.

13. Anthony Summers, *The Arrogance of Power: The Secret World of Richard Nixon* (New York: The Viking Press, 2000), pp. 317–18.

14. Author interview with Terry Murphy, a close Dreyfus associate and preparer of his oral biography, November 14, 2006.

15. Adam Clymer, "Book Offers Peek into Nixon's Mind," *New York Times,* August 27, 2000.

16. Richard Reeves, *President Nixon: Alone in the White House* (New York: Simon and Schuster, 2001), p. 21.

17. Ibid., p. 35.

18. *Diagnostic and Standardized Manual of Mental Disorders,* 4th Ed. (Arlington, Virginia: American Psychiatric Association, 2000), pp. 634–38.

19. Reeves, *President Nixon,* p. 42.

20. Small, *The Presidency of Richard Nixon,* pp. 218–19.

21. Isaacson, *Kissinger,* pp. 149–50.

22. Ibid., p. 146.

23. Ehrlichman, *Witness to Power,* pp. 207–8.

24. Drew, "Washington Report," *Atlantic,* August 1970.

25. Drew, "Washington Report," *Atlantic,* April 1969.

26. Drew, "Washington Report," *Atlantic,* April 1969.

27. Ibid.

28. Ibid., pp. 4–14.

29. Author interview with Christopher De-Muth.

30. Small, *The Presidency of Richard Nixon,* pp. 48–50.

31. Arthur M. Schlesinger Jr., *The Imperial Presidency* (Boston: Houghton Mifflin, 1973), p. 220.

32. Ibid., p. 495.

33. Drew, "Washington Report," *Atlantic,* February 1973.

34. David Gergen, *Eyewitness to Power* (New York: Simon and Schuster, 2000), p. 25.

35. Ehrlichman, *Witness to Power,* p. 79.

36. Marton, *Hidden Power,* p. 171.

37. Small, *The Presidency of Richard Nixon,* p. 224.

38. Gergen, *Eyewitness to Power,* p. 25.

39. Small, *The Presidency of Richard Nixon,* p. 217.

40. H. R. Haldeman, *The Haldeman Diaries: Inside the Nixon White House* (New York: Putnam, 1994), pp. 7–8.

41. Gergen, *Eyewitness to Power,* p. 51.

42. Small, *The Presidency of Richard Nixon,* pp. 217–18.

43. Drew, "Washington Report," *Atlantic,* May 1970.

44. Ibid., p. 22.

45. Richard Nixon, *Leaders* (New York: Warner Books, 1982).

46. Ibid., pp. 42–84.

47. Gergen, *Eyewitness to Power,* pp. 42–45.

48. Drew, "Washington Report," *Atlantic,* April 1973.

49. Evans and Novak, *Nixon in the White House,* p. 110.

50. Richard Nixon, *In the Arena* (New York: Simon and Schuster, 1990), p. 333.

51. Evans and Novak, *Nixon in the White House,* pp. 316–17.

52. Greenberg, *Nixon's Shadow,* p. 158.

53. Ibid., p. 155.

54. Ibid., p. 127.

55. Nixon, *In the Arena,* p. 247.

56. Gergen, *Eyewitness to Power,* p. 54.

57. Greenberg, *Nixon's Shadow,* p. 154.

58. Small, *The Presidency of Richard Nixon,* p. 230.

59. Drew, "Washington Report," *Atlantic,* May 1969.

60. Evans and Novak, *Nixon in the White House,* p. 328.

61. Small, *The Presidency of Richard Nixon,* p. 86.

62. Evans and Novak, *Nixon in the White House,* p. 319.

63. John Osborne, *The Second Year of the Nixon Watch* (New York: Liveright, 1971), p. 171.

64. Evans and Novak, *Nixon in the White House,* pp. 334–39.

65. Small, *The Presidency of Richard Nixon,* pp. 248–49.

66. Evans and Novak, *Nixon in the White House,* p. 345.

67. Osborne, *The Second Year of the Nixon Watch,* p. 177.

68. Drew, "Washington Report," *Atlantic,* May 1970.

69. Ehrlichman, *Witness to Power,* pp. 111–12.

70. Evans and Novak, *Nixon in the White House,* pp. 277–85.

71. Ibid., p. 359.

72. Small, *The Presidency of Richard Nixon,* pp. 41–42.

73. Greenberg, *Nixon's Shadow,* p. 47n.

74. Evans and Novak, *Nixon in the White House,* pp. 34–35.

75. Drew, "Washington Report," *Atlantic,* January 1969.

76. Haldeman, *The Haldeman Diaries,* p. 502.

77. Ibid., p. 187.

78. Small, *The Presidency of Richard Nixon,* p. 173.

79. Ibid., pp. 173–74.

80. Evans and Novak, *Nixon in the White House,* pp. 175–76.

81. Small, *The Presidency of Richard Nixon,* pp. 161–70; author's contemporary reporting.

82. Linda Greenhouse, *Becoming Justice Blackmun* (New York: Times Books, 2005), p. 83.

83. Small, *The Presidency of Richard Nixon,* p. 225.

84. Elizabeth Drew, *Washington Journal: The Events of 1973–1974* (New York: Random House, 1974), p. 6.

85. Reeves, *President Nixon,* p. 35.

86. Evans and Novak, *Nixon in the White House,* p. 4.

CHAPTER FOUR: THE PRAGMATIST

1. Drew, "Washington Report," *Atlantic,* November 1969.
2. Ehrlichman, *Witness to Power,* pp. 212–20.
3. Greenberg, *Nixon's Shadow,* p. 308.
4. Nixon, *In the Arena,* pp. 332–33.
5. Small, *The Presidency of Richard Nixon,* p. 214.
6. Greenberg, *Nixon's Shadow,* p. 108.
7. Wills, *Nixon Agonistes,* p. 558.
8. Drew, "Washington Report," *Atlantic,* March 1967.
9. Drew, "Washington Report," *Atlantic,* January 1973.
10. Small, *The Presidency of Richard Nixon,* p. 155.
11. Drew, "Washington Report," *Atlantic,* November 1969.
12. Osborne, *First Year of the Nixon Watch,* p. 53.
13. Wills, *Nixon Agonistes,* p. 547.
14. Ibid., p. 432.
15. Small, *The Presidency of Richard Nixon,* p. 216.
16. Wills, *Nixon Agonistes,* p. 582.
17. Evans and Novak, *Nixon in the White House,* p. 44.

18. Author interview with Christopher De-Muth.

19. Osborne, *The Nixon Watch,* p. 53.

20. Evans and Novak, *Nixon in the White House,* p. 409.

21. Small, *The Presidency of Richard Nixon,* p. 156.

22. Ehrlichman, *Witness to Power,* p. 317.

23. Small, *The Presidency of Richard Nixon,* p. 242.

24. Reeves, *President Nixon,* p. 163.

25. Small, *The Presidency of Richard Nixon,* p. 197.

26. Ehrlichman, *Witness to Power,* p. 208.

27. Bill Christofferson, *The Man from Clear Lake: Earth Day Founder Senator Gaylord Nelson* (Madison: University of Wisconsin Press, 2004), pp. 213–18.

28. Jonathan Aitken, *Nixon: A Life* (Washington: Regnery Publishing, 1993), p. 397.

29. Christofferson, *Man from Clear Lake,* pp. 327–29.

30. Evans and Novak, *Nixon in the White House,* pp. 213–14.

31. Ibid., p. 224.

32. Haldeman, *The Haldeman Diaries,* p. 181.

33. Evans and Novak, *Nixon in the White*

House, pp. 236–37.

34. Small, *The Presidency of Richard Nixon,* pp. 190–94.
35. Ibid., pp. 100–101.
36. Ibid., p. 208.
37. Drew, "Washington Report," *Atlantic,* May 1970.
38. Richard Nixon, *RN: The Memoirs of President Nixon* (New York: Simon and Schuster, 1990), p. 521.
39. Small, *The Presidency of Richard Nixon,* pp. 203, 208.

CHAPTER FIVE: THE FOREIGN POLICY PRESIDENT

1. Isaacson, *Kissinger,* p. 168.
2. Ibid., p. 132.
3. Small, *The Presidency of Richard Nixon,* p. 54.
4. Ibid., pp. 54–55.
5. Stanley Karnow, *Vietnam: A History* (New York: The Viking Press, 1983), p. 395.
6. Small, *The Presidency of Richard Nixon,* p. 60.
7. Isaacson, *Kissinger,* p. 70.
8. Small, *The Presidency of Richard Nixon,* p. 60.
9. Isaacson, *Kissinger,* p. 364.
10. Ibid., pp. 150–51.

11. Karnow, *Vietnam,* p. 593.

12. Elizabeth Drew, "Exiting Vietnam," *Smithsonian,* March 2003, p. 123.

13. Karnow, *Vietnam,* p. 593.

14. H. R. Haldeman with Joseph DiMona, *The Ends of Power* (New York: Times Books, 1978), pp. 82–83.

15. Scott D. Sagan and Jeremi Suri, "The Madman Nuclear Alert: Secrecy, Signaling, and Safety in October 1969," *International Security* (Cambridge: President and Fellows of Harvard College and the Massachusetts Institute of Technology, 2003), pp. 150–83.

16. Isaacson, *Kissinger,* p. 246.

17. Ibid., pp. 246–48.

18. Karnow, *Vietnam,* pp. 602–3.

19. Isaacson, *Kissinger,* p. 213.

20. Karnow, *Vietnam,* p. 591.

21. Isaacson, *Kissinger,* p. 174.

22. Ibid., pp. 212–17.

23. Drew, "Exiting Vietnam," p. 125.

24. Isaacson, *Kissinger,* p. 265.

25. Ibid., p. 262.

26. Ibid., p. 259.

27. Henry Kissinger, *White House Years* (Boston: Little, Brown, 1979), pp. 487–89.

28. Small, *The Presidency of Richard Nixon,* p. 78.

29. Isaacson, *Kissinger,* p. 268.

30. Ibid., p. 269.

31. Small, *The Presidency of Richard Nixon,* p. 79.

32. Evans and Novak, *Nixon in the White House,* pp. 289–90.

33. Karnow, *Vietnam,* pp. 629–30.

34. Isaacson, *Kissinger,* p. 328.

35. Karnow, *Vietnam,* p. 633.

36. Haldeman, *The Ends of Power,* p. 79.

37. Isaacson, *Kissinger,* p. 441.

38. Karnow, *Vietnam,* p. 650.

39. Isaacson, *Kissinger,* pp. 458–59.

40. Ibid., p. 459.

41. Ibid., pp. 471–75.

42. Ibid., p. 489.

43. John Lewis Gaddis, *The Long Peace: Inquiries into the History of the Cold War* (New York: Oxford University Press, 1987), p. 165.

44. John Lewis Gaddis, *The Cold War: A New History* (New York: The Penguin Press, 2005), pp. 149–51.

45. Small, *The Presidency of Richard Nixon,* p. 100.

46. Isaacson, *Kissinger,* p. 169.

47. Avis Bohlen, "The Rise and Fall of Arms Control," *Survival* (International Institute for Strategic Studies, Autumn 2003), p. 9.

48. Isaacson, *Kissinger,* p. 403.

49. Small, *The Presidency of Richard Nixon,* p. 98.
50. Ibid., p. 102.
51. Gerard Smith, *Doubletalk* (New York: Doubleday, 1980), p. 376.
52. Isaacson, *Kissinger,* pp. 410–15.
53. Small, *The Presidency of Richard Nixon,* p. 112.
54. Henry Kissinger, *Years of Upheaval* (Boston: Little, Brown, 1982), p. 549.
55. Isaacson, *Kissinger,* pp. 350–51.
56. Small, *The Presidency of Richard Nixon,* p. 123.
57. Gaddis, *The Cold War,* pp. 151–52.
58. Isaacson, *Kissinger,* p. 404.
59. Ibid., p. 511.
60. Ibid., p. 522.
61. Ibid., pp. 474–75.
62. Ibid., pp. 530–32.
63. Small, *The Presidency of Richard Nixon,* pp. 139–40.
64. Isaacson, *Kissinger,* p. 373.
65. Small, *The Presidency of Richard Nixon,* p. 142.

CHAPTER SIX: WATERGATE

1. Drew, *Washington Journal,* p. 11.
2. Ibid., pp. 12–13.
3. Ibid., p. 144.
4. Reeves, *President Nixon,* p. 101.

5. Ibid.

6. Author interview with Leslie Gelb.

7. Stanley I. Kutler, *The Wars of Watergate: The Last Crisis of Richard Nixon* (New York: Norton, 1992), pp. 113–15.

8. Author interview with Leslie Gelb.

9. Isaacson, *Kissinger,* p. 330.

10. Drew, *Washington Journal,* p. 19.

11. Kutler, *The Wars of Watergate,* p. 107. (This was of a piece with the construction workers, encouraged by the White House, attacking demonstrators in New York in May 1970.)

12. Ibid., pp. 105–6.

13. Drew, *Washington Journal,* pp. 86–88.

14. Small, *The Presidency of Richard Nixon,* pp. 250–55.

15. Eugenio Martinez, *Mission Impossible,* http://www.watergate.info/ burglary/ martinez.shtml.

16. Richard Ben-Veniste and George Frampton Jr., *Stonewall* (New York: Simon and Schuster, 1977), pp. 46–47.

17. Drew, *Washington Journal,* p. 12.

18. Kutler, *The Wars of Watergate,* pp. 204–5.

19. Ben-Veniste and Frampton, *Stonewall,* p. 50.

20. Stanley I. Kutler, *Abuse of Power: The New Nixon Tapes* (New York: Touchstone,

1997), pp. 47–56.

21. Drew, "Washington Report," *Atlantic,* August 1973.

22. Kutler, *The Wars of Watergate,* pp. 263–64.

23. Ibid., p. 268.

24. Kutler, *Abuse of Power,* p. 4.

25. Drew, *Washington Journal,* pp. 141, 229.

26. Ibid., p. 43.

27. Ben-Veniste and Frampton, *Stonewall,* p. 24.

28. Ibid., p. 19.

29. Drew, "Washington Report," *Atlantic,* August 1973.

30. Kutler, *The Wars of Watergate,* p. 280.

31. Haldeman, *The Haldeman Diaries,* p. 525.

32. Drew, "Washington Report," *Atlantic,* April 1969.

33. Kutler, *Abuse of Power,* p. xxii.

34. Drew, *Washington Journal,* pp. 68–69.

35. Ibid., pp. 5–7.

36. Ben-Veniste and Frampton, *Stonewall,* p. 135.

37. Drew, *Washington Journal,* p. 47; Ben-Veniste and Frampton, *Stonewall,* pp. 127–30.

38. Kutler, *The Wars of Watergate,* p. 418.

39. Ben-Veniste and Frampton, *Stonewall,* pp. 126–32.

40. Ibid., pp. 135–37.

41. Drew, *Washington Journal,* p. 52.

42. Ibid., p. 61.

43. Ibid., p. 69.

44. Ibid., p. 41.

45. Ibid., p. 89.

46. Ibid., p. 132.

47. Kutler, *The Wars of Watergate,* p. 218.

48. Drew, *Washington Journal,* p. 228.

49. Ibid., p. 130.

50. Kutler, *The Wars of Watergate,* p. 430.

51. Ibid., p. 447.

52. Ibid., p. 443.

53. Drew, *Washington Journal,* p. 157.

54. Ibid., p. 112.

55. Ibid., p. 167.

56. Author interviews with Rodino assistant Francis O'Brien; and contemporary interviews with Rodino and other members of the committee.

57. Drew, *Washington Journal,* pp. 78–79.

58. Ibid., pp. 188–210.

59. Osborne, *The Nixon Watch,* p. 57.

60. Drew, *Washington Journal,* pp. 248–52.

61. Ibid., p. 315.

62. Ibid., p. 295.

63. Monica Crowley, *Nixon Off the Record* (New York: Random House, 1996), p. 65.

64. Author interview with O'Brien.

65. Kutler, *The Wars of Watergate,* p. 504.

66. Drew, *Washington Journal,* p. 333.
67. Kutler, *The Wars of Watergate,* p. 515.
68. Drew, *Washington Journal,* pp. 363–64.
69. Ibid.
70. Ibid., p. 389.
71. Summers, *The Arrogance of Power,* pp. 478–80; Adam Clymer, "Book Offers Peek into Nixon's Mind," *New York Times,* August 27, 2000.
72. Bob Woodward and Carl Bernstein, *The Final Days* (New York: Simon and Schuster, 1976), p. 421.
73. Ibid., pp. 422–25.
74. Drew, *Washington Journal,* p. 414.

CHAPTER SEVEN: THE WIZARD

1. Robert Sam Anson, *Exile: The Unquiet Oblivion of Richard M. Nixon* (New York: Simon and Schuster, 1984), p. 36.
2. Ibid., p. 53.
3. Ibid., pp. 49–50.
4. Small, *The Presidency of Richard Nixon,* p. 298.
5. Anson, *Exile,* pp. 60–62.
6. Ibid., pp. 67–68.
7. Ibid., pp. 27–32.
8. Ibid., p. 65.
9. Ibid., pp. 34, 73.
10. David Frost, *"I Gave Them a Sword":*

Behind the Scenes of the Nixon Interviews (New York: Morrow, 1978), p. 152.

11. Ibid., pp. 241–42.
12. Author interview with David Frost.
13. Frost, *"I Gave Them a Sword,"* p. 288.
14. Anson, *Exile,* p. 131.
15. Ibid., pp. 195–96.
16. Ibid., pp. 198–201.
17. Ibid., p. 209.
18. Ibid., pp. 218–19.
19. Greenberg, *Nixon's Shadow,* p. 280.
20. Ibid., p. 285.
21. Small, *The Presidency of Richard Nixon,* p. 306.
22. Greenberg, *Nixon's Shadow,* p. 285.
23. Anson, *Exile,* pp. 260–61.
24. Elizabeth Drew, *On the Edge: The Clinton Presidency* (New York: Simon and Schuster, 1994), p. 141.
25. Author interview with Vin Weber, former Republican member of Congress.
26. Anson, *Exile,* p. 227.
27. Ibid., pp. 229–30.
28. Ibid., pp. 238–43.
29. Ibid., p. 269.
30. For an examination of this and other Nixon attempts to gain new stature by manipulating the press, see Marvin Kalb, *The Nixon Memo: Political Respectability, Russia, and the Press* (Chicago: University

of Chicago Press, 1994).

31. Author interview with John Fund.

32. Anson, *Exile,* p. 274.

33. Greenberg, *Nixon's Shadow,* p. 303.

34. Kalb, *Nixon Memo,* p. 138.

35. Small, *The Presidency of Richard Nixon,* pp. 306–7.

36. Author interview with Timothy Naftali, the first director of the reconstituted Nixon Library.

37. See http://nixon.archives.gov/laws/litigation.html.

38. Anson, *Exile,* p. 237.

MILESTONES

1913	Born January 9 in Yorba Linda, California, to Frank and Hannah Milhous Nixon
1930	Graduates from Whittier Union High School
1934	Graduates from Whittier College
1937	Graduates from Duke University School of Law; takes a job in a small Whittier law firm
1940	Marries Thelma "Pat" Ryan on June 21
1942	Works with the Office of Price Administration in Washington, D.C.
1942–45	Serves as a navy lieutenant
1946	Elected to U.S. House of Representatives, defeating Jerry Voorhis

1947	Joins House Un-American Activities Committee
1948	Alger Hiss case
1950	Elected to U.S. Senate, defeating Helen Gahagan Douglas
1952	Nominated as Dwight Eisenhower's vice presidential running mate
	Responds to corruption allegations in Checkers speech
	Elected vice president
1954	Geneva Accords ends French colonial era in Vietnam
1956	"Dump Nixon" movement
1959	Debates Soviet leader Nikita Khrushchev in Moscow (Kitchen Debate)
1960	Compact of Fifth Avenue with Nelson Rockefeller
	Kennedy–Nixon debates
	Loses presidential election to John F. Kennedy
1962	Runs for governor of California but is defeated by Edmund G. "Pat" Brown; holds "last press conference"
1963	Moves to New York
	Publishes *Six Crises*
1966	Campaigns for Republican congressional candidates

1968	Affirms a "secret plan" to end the Vietnam War
	Receives Republican nomination for president and selects Spiro T. Agnew as running mate
	As election nears, President Johnson announces total cessation of bombing of North Vietnam, and South Vietnamese reject meeting in Paris with representatives of the Vietcong
	Wins presidential election, defeating Hubert H. Humphrey
1969	Travels to Europe on first foreign trip as president
	Issues orders directing private political funds for secret White House intelligence operations
	Endorses Anti–Ballistic Missile Treaty in expanded form
	Begins secret bombing of Cambodia
	Strategic Arms Limitation Talks begin
	Proposes the Family Assistance Plan

Secretly orders a worldwide nuclear alert, lasting a month, to frighten the Soviets into pressing the North Vietnamese to make concessions in the Paris talks

Senate rejects Supreme Court nominee Clement Haynsworth

1970   Signs the National Environmental Protection Act

Henry Kissinger begins secret meetings in Paris with North Vietnamese foreign minister Le Duc Tho

Senate rejects Supreme Court nominee G. Harrold Carswell; Harry Blackmun later confirmed

Earth Day

Announces military "incursion" into Cambodia

National Guard kills four students at Kent State University, Ohio

Visits antiwar demonstrators at Lincoln Memorial

Institutes a ninety-day freeze on wages and prices

Fires Secretary of the Interior Walter Hickel

Welcomes Elvis Presley to White House

1971 Chinese government invites U.S. Ping-Pong team to play in China

New York Times begins publishing the Pentagon Papers

John Ehrlichman sets up "plumbers" operation

White House team breaks into office of Dr. Lewis Fielding, psychiatrist of Daniel Ellsberg

1972 Visits the People's Republic of China; Shanghai Communiqué issued

First summit meeting with Soviet leader Leonid Brezhnev

Signs the Clean Water Act

Five arrested on June 17 in burglary at DNC headquarters in the Watergate office building

Talks to John Dean on June 21 about getting money to pay off the Watergate burglars

Discusses with H. R. Haldeman on June 23 having the CIA ask the FBI to halt its investigation of the Watergate break-in

Watergate burglars indicted by grand jury

Renominated for a second term; defeats George McGovern in general election

Christmas bombing of North Vietnam

1973   Announces a Vietnam cease-fire; Paris Peace Accords signed; the last American troops are withdrawn from Vietnam

John Dean describes the Watergate cover-up as a "cancer on the presidency"

Watergate burglars sentenced

Nominates Elliot Richardson to be attorney general

Richardson selects Archibald Cox as independent counsel

Ehrlichman and Haldeman resign; Dean is fired

Senate Select Committee on Presidential Campaign Activities commences public hearings into the Watergate affair

John Mitchell indicted along with key Nixon fund-raisers

Nixon–Brezhnev summit in California

Alexander Butterfield reveals existence of White House taping system

Chilean president Salvador Allende overthrown, with encouragement of the United States

Yom Kippur War

Spiro Agnew pleads nolo contendere to bribery charge and resigns as vice president and submits his resignation

Announces his selection of Gerald Ford as new vice president

Saturday Night Massacre; fires Cox; Richardson resigns

Kissinger receives the Nobel Peace Prize

1974	Grand jury indicts Ehrlichman, Haldeman, Mitchell, Colson, and others for conspiracy in the Watergate cover-up
	Nixon–Brezhnev summit in Moscow
	Supreme Court rules unanimously that the president has to surrender the Watergate tapes
	House Judiciary Committee approves three articles of impeachment
	Announces resignation on August 8; leaves office the following day
	President Ford pardons Nixon on September 8
	Congress rules that all of Nixon's presidential papers and tapes belong to the federal government
1975	End of Vietnam War; fall of Saigon
1976	Travels to China as a private citizen
1977	David Frost interviews
1978	Publishes *RN, his memoirs*
1980	Moves to New York

1981	Attends funerals of the Shah of Iran and Egyptian president Anwar Sadat
1990	Nixon Library opens in Yorba Linda
1993	Death of Pat Nixon on June 22
1994	Dies of a stroke on April 22

SELECTED BIBLIOGRAPHY

BOOKS

Aitken, Jonathan. *Nixon: A Life.* Washington, D.C.: Regnery, 1993.

Anson, Robert Sam. *Exile: The Unquiet Oblivion of Richard Nixon.* New York: Simon and Schuster, 1984.

Ben-Veniste, Richard, and George Frampton Jr. *Stonewall: The Real Story of the Watergate Prosecution.* New York: Simon and Schuster, 1977.

Christian, George. *The President Steps Down: A Personal Memoir of the Transfer of Power.* New York: Macmillan, 1970.

Cohen, Richard, and Jules Witcover. *A Heartbeat Away: The Investigation & Resignation of Vice President Spiro T. Agnew.* New York: The Viking Press, 1974.

Crowley, Monica. *Nixon Off the Record: His Candid Commentary on People and Politics.* New York: Random House, 1996.

Dean, John. *Blind Ambition: The White House Years.* New York: Simon and Schuster, 1976.

Drew, Elizabeth. *On the Edge: The Clinton Presidency.* New York: Simon and Schuster, 1994.

——. *Washington Journal: The Events of 1973–1974.* New York: Random House, 1974.

Ehrlichman, John. *Witness to Power: The Nixon Years.* New York: Simon and Schuster, 1982.

Eisenhower, Julie Nixon. *Pat Nixon: The Untold Story.* New York: Simon and Schuster, 1983.

Evans, Rowland, Jr., and Robert D. Novak. *Nixon in the White House: The Frustration of Power.* New York: Random House, 1971.

Frost, David. *"I Gave Them a Sword": Behind the Scenes of the Nixon Interviews.* New York: William Morrow, 1978.

Gaddis, John Lewis. *The Cold War: A New History.* New York: The Penguin Press, 2005.

——. *The Long Peace: Inquiries into the History of the Cold War.* New York: Oxford University Press, 1987.

Garment, Leonard. *Crazy Rhythm: From*

Brooklyn and Jazz to Nixon's White House, Watergate, and Beyond. New York: Perseus, 2001.

Gellman, Irwin F. *The Contender: Richard Nixon, The Congress Years, 1946–1952.* New York: Free Press, 1999.

Gergen, David. *Eyewitness to Power: The Essence of Leadership, Nixon to Clinton.* New York: Simon and Schuster, 2000.

Greenberg, David. *Nixon's Shadow: The History of an Image.* New York: W. W. Norton, 2004.

Haldeman, H. R. *The Haldeman Diaries: Inside the Nixon White House.* New York: G. P. Putnam's Sons, 1994.

Hutschnecker, Arnold. *The Drive for Power.* New York: M. Evans, 1974.

Isaacson, Walter. *Kissinger: A Biography.* New York: Simon and Schuster, 1992.

Karnow, Stanley. *Vietnam: A History.* New York: The Viking Press, 1983.

Kissinger, Henry. *White House Years.* Boston: Little, Brown, 1979.

——. *Years of Upheaval.* Boston: Little, Brown, 1982.

Kutler, Stanley. *Abuse of Power: The New Nixon Tapes.* New York: Touchstone, 1997.

——. *The Wars of Watergate: The Last Crisis*

of *Richard Nixon.* New York: W. W. Norton, 1992.

Lewis, Chris, and Godfrey Hodgson. *An American Melodrama: The Presidential Campaign of 1968.* New York: The Viking Press, 1969.

Mankiewicz, Frank. *Perfectly Clear: Nixon from Whittier to Watergate.* New York: Quadrangle, 1973.

Marton, Kati. *Hidden Power: The Presidential Marriages That Shaped Our Recent History.* New York: Pantheon Books, 2001.

Morris, Roger. *Richard Milhous Nixon: The Rise of an American Politician.* New York: Henry Holt, 1990.

Nixon, Richard M. *Leaders.* New York: Touchstone, 1990.

———. *RN: The Memoirs of Richard Nixon.* New York: Grosset and Dunlap, 1978.

———. *Six Crises.* New York: Doubleday, 1962.

Osborne, John. *The Fourth Year of the Nixon Watch.* New York: Liveright, 1973.

———. *The Third Year of the Nixon Watch.* New York: Liveright, 1972.

———. *The Second Year of the Nixon Watch.* New York: Liveright, 1971.

———. *The Nixon Watch.* New York: Liveright, 1970.

Phillips, Kevin. *The Emerging Republican Majority.* New Rochelle, N.Y.: Arlington House, 1969.

Reeves, Richard. *President Nixon: Alone in the White House.* New York: Simon and Schuster, 2001.

Reeves, Thomas. *The Life and Times of Joe McCarthy.* New York: Stein and Day, 1982.

Safire, William. *Before the Fall: An Inside View of the Pre-Watergate White House.* New York: Doubleday, 1975.

Schlesinger, Arthur M., Jr. *The Imperial Presidency.* Boston: Houghton Mifflin, 1973.

Small, Melvin. *The Presidency of Richard Nixon.* Lawrence, Kans.: University Press of Kansas, 1999.

Smith, Gerard. *Doubletalk: The Story of SALT I.* Garden City, N.Y.: Doubleday, 1980.

Summers, Anthony. *The Arrogance of Power: The Secret World of Richard Nixon.* New York: The Viking Press, 2000.

White, Theodore H. *The Making of the President, 1960.* New York: Atheneum, 1961.

Wicker, Tom. *One of Us: Richard Nixon and the American Dream.* New York: Random House, 1991.

Woodward, Bob, and Carl Bernstein. *The Final Days.* New York: Simon and Schuster, 1976.

Articles

Bohlen, Avis. "The Rise and Fall of Arms Control." *Survival* (International Institute for Strategic Studies), Autumn 2003.

Clymer, Adam, "Book Offers Peek into Nixon's Mind." *New York Times,* August 27, 2000.

Drew, Elizabeth. "Exiting Vietnam." *Smithsonian,* March 2003.

——. "Washington Report." *Atlantic,* August 1973.

——. "Washington Report." *Atlantic,* May 1971.

——. "Washington Report." *Atlantic,* October 1970.

——. "Washington Report." *Atlantic,* August 1970.

——. "Washington Report." *Atlantic,* May 1970.

——. "Washington Report." *Atlantic,* November 1969.

——. "Washington Report." *Atlantic,* May 1969.

——. "Washington Report." *Atlantic,* April 1969.

——. "Washington Report." *Atlantic,* January 1969.

——. "Washington Report." *Atlantic,* March 1967.

Sagan, Scott, and Jeremi Suri, "The Madman Nuclear Alert: Secrecy, Signaling, and Safety in October 1969." *International Security,* Spring 2003.

Stout, David. "2 Nixon Aides Skeptical About Report That He Took Drug." *New York Times,* August 31, 2000.

Tanenhaus, Sam. "Mud Wrestling." (Review of *Tricky Dick and the Pink Lady: Richard Nixon vs. Helen Gahagan Douglas — Sexual Politics and the Red Scare, 1950* by Greg Mitchell.) *New York Times Book Review,* February 1, 1998.

ACKNOWLEDGMENTS

It is more than appropriate to dedicate this book to a giant of our times, and also a dear friend, who recently left us: Arthur M. Schlesinger, Jr. Arthur was exceptional and extraordinary — a shining intellect, icon of historians, and a kind and generous man. For countless people, he was also one of the most engaging individuals that they have ever known. He honored me with his friendship for many years, and was an inspiration to all who wanted to understand history. Though he was the general editor of the American Presidents series, he was the first to admit, with his usual grace, that he didn't initially think of me to write the book on Richard Nixon, but after that he was an enthusiastic supporter and steady encourager. Fortunately, he was able the read this book before it was published.

When, out of the blue, Paul Golob, the editorial director of Times Books, first approached me about writing this book, I was surprised, honored — and found the idea irresistible. Here was an opportunity to reexamine, from a further distance, one of the most complex and interesting presidents in American history. Given the brevity of the books in this series, I had to pick and choose among the treasure trove of new information published after Nixon's presidency — and his postpresidency. I read and was tempted by far more than could be included in the condensed Nixon, and so if others' work is not mentioned in the footnotes, that does not signify that their contributions were not worthy of interest or respect.

In fact, the requirement to present the condensed Nixon helped me get to what I saw as his essence; to see him in new ways; and, I think, to finally understand him.

So that makes me particularly grateful to Paul for thinking of me to write this book. Beyond that, he was a steady supporter, provided a fine mind that could quickly grasp and respond to my ideas about how to proceed, and whose editorial skill greatly helped me improve the manuscript.

Two other people also deserve special acknowledgment. Very much on my mind as I worked on this book were two extraordinary mentors who inspired, taught, and encouraged me as I wrote and thought about Nixon. The first was the late William Shawn, the editor of the *New Yorker* during seventeen of my years there, who invited me to write a series on Nixon's turbulence and possible downfall. He was an exacting but exceptionally kindly man, one who gave his writers confidence (which every writer longs for) even as he stretched us, and, speaking for myself, got better work out of me than I thought I was, or had been, capable of doing. The second was the late John W. Gardner, the founder of Common Cause among other things, who gave me guidance and insights that expanded my understanding of the world around us, as well as shrewd advice and moral support.

I am also grateful to some people whom I consulted for their expertise in certain subjects covered in this book. What I drew from their advice is my responsibility, not theirs, but they all generously offered important guidance. They are: Scott Armstrong, Avis Bohlen, William Brenner, Christopher DeMuth, Jim Dickenson, Peter Edelman, Sir David Frost, John Fund, Leslie Gelb, Timothy Naftali, Dr. Judith Nowak, Alice Rivlin, Charles Schultze, Strobe Talbott. And there are two people who were indispensable to my writing this book: Mariel Villegas, who helped me while completing her college studies, proved to be unusually smart, was wise beyond her years, and, best of all, cracked me up with her humor. My friend and confidante Tessie Villegas held me and our household together.

ABOUT THE AUTHOR

Elizabeth Drew is the award-winning author of thirteen previous books, including *Washington Journal, Politics and Money, Whatever It Takes: The Real Struggle for Political Power in America,* and *The Corruption of American Politics.* She is a regular political correspondent for the *New York Review of Books* and the former Washington correspondent for *The New Yorker.* She lives and works in Washington, D.C.